CANALS

THE MAKING
OF A NATION

CANALS

THE MAKING OF A NATION

A JOURNEY INTO THE HEART OF INDUSTRIAL BRITAIN

LIZ McIVOR

BOOKS

1 3 5 7 9 10 8 6 4 2

BBC Books, an imprint of Ebury Publishing
20 Vauxhall Bridge Road,
London SW1V 2SA

BBC Books is part of the Penguin Random House group of companies
whose addresses can be found at global.penguinrandomhouse.com

Penguin
Random House
UK

This book is published to accompany the television series entitled
Canals: The Making of a Nation first broadcast on BBC One in 2015.

Executive producer: Tony Parker
Series producer: Andy Richards
Producers: Ed Barlow, Stuart Woodman, Paul Craven.
Researchers: Vicky Spratt, Georgia Plimbley, Rehannah Mian, Victoria Stanley

First published by BBC Books in 2015

www.eburypublishing.co.uk

A CIP catalogue record for this book is available from the British Library

ISBN 9781849901086

Printed and bound in Great Britain by Clays Ltd, St Ives PLC

For my Father, Terence.

Thanks for being that most inspiring
of characters, an interested man.

CONTENTS

INTRODUCTION

I am writing the introduction to this book at the end of the process, which, I am told, is the usual way of going about things in the publishing world. In the normal process of reading and writing about history, although we generally start with an event, a point in time, a pivotal moment by which we can spot a change and mark time, the same is ultimately true. When thinking about the impact of a major event in the history of our country, and the world in general (for example, the Battle of Trafalgar), it is rarely that a historian or indeed anyone else wakes up in the morning and asks themselves, 'How did the Battle of Trafalgar directly affect me and the people of the town I live in?' It doesn't happen that way. Inevitably, a person asks questions first about the things they already know and then tracks back to try to understand them better. A man waking up opposite a naval dockyard in the United Kingdom might see a reconstruction of an early nineteenth-century ship and wonder how it is that this thing was built here, or a tourist might walk through Trafalgar Square and take a passing glance at Nelson's Column. Usually, it is what people see and come into contact with that sparks their interest in and enthusiasm for finding out more about something that, in some way, directly or indirectly affects them.

As a child I was always interested in history; not just in British history, and not just the modern, and to be honest it was something of an obsession. Former schoolteachers would be able to attest to this by virtue of the confiscation of numerous history textbooks from under the desks during maths lessons. The particular link for me was being able to be in direct contact with a thing from the past, an object used or made by a real person long gone, or being able to stand literally in the footsteps of those who lived in a home, built a monument or worked in a location every day of their lives. This was what drew me to museum work, beyond the academic remit of the archive and the library. For me the wealth of experience was in real, tangible things. It was through access to places, buildings and objects that I was better able to see myself in the shoes of people from history, to imagine how they lived and worked, what they thought and how they felt about their lives and the events they lived through. This has been the overriding enjoyment of the task of working on the television series and writing the accompanying book.

My first brush with the canals was visiting the relatively rural village of Marple, south of Manchester, walking along the towpath of the Peak Forest Canal with my family in the 1980s. At that time, work to restore and improve that particular stretch of canal was under way and, although local parks were magnets for urban families on a bank holiday Monday, there was little along the towpath to explain to the uninitiated what was there and why. The impressive aqueduct and the spectacular scenery of the Goyt Valley were inspiring enough, but they raised a question: why and how could such a structure be built through the dramatic landscape? My dad was the one who was interested in such things and enthused about days gone by when tough men would have been working the route from Derbyshire. Learning about the Industrial Revolution at school – and the obligatory lessons about the revolution in transport – focused on another local route, the Bridgewater, arguably the first modern canal to kick-start the game of canal building in the late eighteenth century.

The fame of this inland waterway, opened in 1761, derived from an extraordinary feat: cutting a man-made trench through the land from one point to another to 'navigate' without following an existing river. It was built to lower costs, exploiting a market for coal and making considerable profits in a new industrial age, and it heralded a wave of canal building in England. The third Duke of Bridgewater,

Francis Egerton, put an idea of his father's into practice at a young age, having observed the effectiveness of continental waterways and being aware of the use of 'navigations' along existing waterways.

James Brindley, the engineer who made it happen, became famous, too, and his expertise was brought to bear on other early industrial waterways, which are still with us today. The technology behind the construction and operation of locks was an old idea, but the size and scale of the eighteenth-century developments would astound the British population and greatly increase the potential for linking up the regions to share the Industrial Revolution which created modern Britain.

Other individuals involved with canal building became equally famous for the ways they solved problems, built impressive structures and changed the way the modern world was to operate. Many more are forgotten by history and remain obscure to the millions of people who enjoy the canals and rivers today.

The age of the canal was short, curtailed by the arrival of the railways in the first half of the nineteenth century. Not all the canals that were built were commercially successful, but they represented change on a massive scale and provided the expertise and ambition to push technological as well as social boundaries. The canals were breeding grounds for the invention and innovation which would provide the country with professionally qualified experts in the fields of science and engineering. They would later become a world apart where those who worked them developed a lifestyle and culture of their own.

Understanding that there was a link between the physical landscape of the city and the way it might have looked beforehand was a bridge to understanding both what had gone before and what was to follow. In this sense, the canal story illustrated perfectly what a monumental change had occurred in Britain in such a short space of time. Growing up in Manchester as I did, the canals, however important in history and culture, were usually the butt of jokes, and mentioned in thinly veiled threats and scare stories. For most of my classmates the canals around the city were places you could go to get drunk, have fights or, if you were unlucky, to be mugged, certainly not respectable leisure or recreation hot spots. How this has changed. Where once there were overgrown towpaths and abandoned supermarket trolleys, today the urban centre, partly built around the canal routes, hosts waterfront bars, clubs, apartments and hotels. What is more, they are once again the home of boats, for hire, leisure cruise and permanent dwelling. In the post-industrial city, an aspect of its earliest days lives on and has been partly responsible for the urban regeneration of hundreds of warehouses, factories and commercial buildings.

For me the story of the canals is one not just of the development of cities like my home town, but of the connection to other regions, the way industry, and with it culture and identity, has been shaped over the 200 or more years since they were built. The Industrial Revolution represented a change in almost every aspect of people's lives in a very short space of time, and in some ways is something that British people continue to adjust to today. Apart from the development of regional specialism in trade, and the special character of the towns, cities and countryside the canals pass through, the waterways interpret themselves. Unlike roads and railways, the canals are relatively timeless. The way people travel them (although today by diesel and electric motor rather than by horsepower) is the same; most of the craft used and the technology encountered serve as a kind of living museum to an era of 'busyness'.

Although never designed with the intention of being a 'network', canals gradually were brought to link up and form the very first long-distance haulage system inland. The remaining canals, the ones which were completed and which have been restored for use, are a snapshot of success. The success of the system is arguably small, as most lines were profitable for a relatively short period of time compared to the effort and investment applied to their construction.

So, bearing in mind their regional focus around important industries, and the fact that they did not spread to every city and region in the country, might lead to the question: what did the canals really do for us? During the course of this project, a number of themes were explored to answer that question. Did the canals do more for us and have a longer-lasting impact than the purpose for which they were originally intended? I believe the answer is that they did, and that, apart from the obvious urban expansion and prompting of the development of faster, cheaper and more efficient transport networks like railways, they gave us so much more. Canals, the people who campaigned for them, about them and those who studied them, enabled a better understanding of how things worked, and how new technology could be made to do more for ordinary people. They developed a network between regions, a communication between towns and cities which didn't exist before. Through this network, people moved and met others, relocated, were able to buy fuel, raw materials and luxury goods. Ultimately, this development changed people's environments, expectations, and, ultimately, their lives.

I also had to ask myself the question: 'What did the canals do for me?' In the first place, they offered me a personal window to the past on my own doorstep, a use of them which was associated with pleasant childhood memories, and later an understanding that these networks, the digging of them and the rapid expansion which they fostered, and which would later put them out of business, was partly what brought, by degrees, my own family to the city of Manchester as it did thousands, indeed millions, of others to industrial centres around the United Kingdom. These were places where there were jobs and the opportunity to build new lives, but most importantly to do so in order that those who would come afterwards might have a better life and a choice about how to make their way.

This book is not intended to be either a full and concise history of the selected regional waterways, or an academic treatment of social influence or capitalist economies in the UK. The history of English canals alone is a vast and complex subject, and no one book could ever hope to tell the story fully. For those who wish to examine the subject, the individual routes and the many canal companies, there are countless authors, archives and academics to consult. This book is intended to be a gentle way in for those who are interested in British history and culture and who may have been inspired by the view, wishing for just a little more. Some readers may disagree with some of the viewpoints, but while this is not written with the academic in mind it is also worth noting that history is but an interpretation of what remains, and will therefore always be subject to interpretation and revision. There is no definitive 'truth', only an attempt at understanding and empathizing with people and times which we can never hope to understand fully.

I hope readers will find their own inspiration from the following as much as I have in compiling it, and that people will continue to make use of and enjoy these waterways and the unique stories associated with them.

CANALS AND NAVIGABLE RIVERS OF ENGLAND AND WALES

1. Lancaster Canal
2. Leeds & Liverpool: Springs Branch
3. Ripon Canal
4. Pocklington Canal
5. Driffield Navigation
6. Market Weighton Canal
7. Selby Canal
8. Aire & Calder Navigation
9. Calder & Hebble Navigation
10. Ribble Link
11. Leeds & Liverpool: Rufford Branch
12. Leeds & Liverpool Canal
13. Rochdale Canal
14. Huddersfield Broad Canal
15. New Junction Canal
16. Sheffield & South Yorkshire Navigation
17. Huddersfield Narrow Canal
18. Ashton Canal
19. Leeds & Liverpool: Leigh Branch
20. Manchester Ship Canal
21. Bridgewater Canal
22. Peak Forest Canal
23. Macclesfield Canal
24. Chesterfield Canal
25. Witham Navigable Drains
26. Kyme Eau: Sleaford Navigation
27. Erewash Canal
28. Trent & Mersey: Leek Branch
29. Trent & Mersey: Caldon Branch
30. Shropshire Union: Llangollen Canal
31. Montgomery Canal
32. Shropshire Union Canal
33. Trent & Mersey Canal
34. Grantham Canal
35. Grand Union: Leicester Branch
36. Ashby Canal
37. Birmingham & Fazley Canal
38. Wyrley & Essington Canal
39. Staffordshire & Worcestershire Canal
40. Droitwich Canal
41. Worcester & Birmingham Canal
42. Stratford upon Avon Canal
43. Coventry Canal
44. Oxford Canal (North)
45. Grand Union: Market Harborough Branch
46. Grand Union: Welford Branch
47. Middle Level Navigations
48. Grand Union: Northampton Branch
49. Grand Union Canal
50. Grand Union: Aylesbury Branch
51. Thames & Severn Canal
52. Stroudwater Canal
53. Gloucester & Sharpness Ship Canal
54. Monmouthshire & Brecon Canal
55. Bridgewater & Taunton Canal
56. Kennet & Avon Canal
57. Basingstoke Canal
58. Grand Union: Slough Branch
59. Grand Union: Paddington Branch
60. Regent's Canal

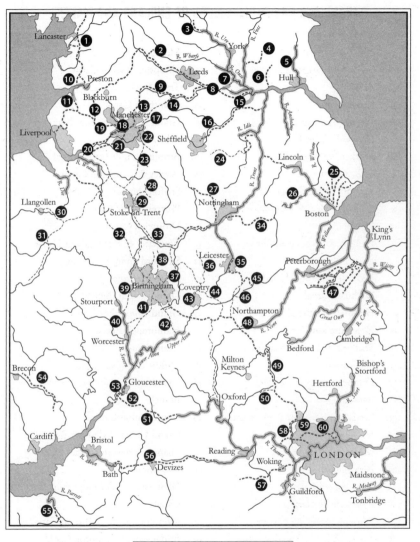

1

THE NEW
CAPITALISM:
LONDON

IMAGINE A MEDIEVAL MERCHANT arriving at the outskirts of the city at somewhere like Chelsea or Islington. The first things he would have noticed would have been the noise, the smell and the overcrowding. He would have met more people in his first hour there than he had ever seen in his own town or village. Here were the grandest houses, the most heavily congested streets and the most voracious market places, all in one tiny area. Travellers from all over the world would be cutting deals in the streets, eating and drinking and looking for ale and a bed after the day's work was done. London today is some 541 times the size in square miles than it was in the fourteenth century but, even then, the capital was a large urban area, its population young, ethnically diverse, more likely to be in work, and competing for space.

Southwark lies south of London Bridge. Fronting the River Thames, it was used as a defensive point. The 'South Walk' provided access to the bridge by foot, which is why the pilgrims of Chaucer's *Canterbury Tales* meet at the Tabard Inn ready for their long journey to the Shrine of St Thomas Beckett in Kent.

> *Bifel that in that sesoun on one day*
> *In Southwerk at the Tabard, as I lay,*
> *Redy to wenden on my pilgrimage,*
> *To Caunterbury with full devout corage,*
> *At night was come into that hostelry,*
> *Wel nine and twenty in a compaignye.*
>
> (Geoffrey Chaucer, General Prologue, *The Canterbury Tales*)

The 1684 'Frost Fair', held on the River Thames in front of London Bridge. During the late 17th and 18th centuries, during what some have termed the 'little ice age', the Thames was prone to freezing over. This made the vital trading link unpredictable, and tidal surges could make it dangerous to navigate.

The Tabard was just one of many hostelries which filled the area to provide shelter and meals for hundreds and thousands of visitors. An inn was a reasonably genteel establishment compared to the common alehouse and more like a boarding house. Here the landlord was obliged to look to the safety of his guests as well as their comforts. These places would be a 'home from home' where deals could be done and legal papers witnessed.

Although a medieval traveller could be reasonably secure in the walls of his lodging, the immediate area was known for being rough and ready. Southwark was home to all the entertainments that a dock worker or a boatman might want, from bear-baiting arenas to brothels and stews, and even that most unsanitary and low of entertainments, the theatre. There was something for everyone 'south of the water'. This was the spot upon which the Elizabethan theatres were built in the round; the audience could participate in the atmosphere of the action, call out to the actors, and throw items on to the stage.

As well as these paid entertainments of 'low degree', there was a high incidence of crime, especially from the waterside. The area was also the site of choice for the punishment of criminals. It was considered best if a potential thief could be reminded of consequences in his own locality. The local 'Clink' and Marshalsea prisons and other lockups known as 'Bridewells' were not intended to house common criminals, but were a system for recovering debts. A person imprisoned for debt would be expected gradually to pay off what he owed or be declared bankrupt by the courts. More prisons and workhouses opened up, because where there was an opportunity to make easy money, trouble would always be attracted. Murder, theft and even petty crimes could carry a death sentence. The heads displayed by London Bridge (usually those of notorious criminals and state traitors) were easily seen from the inns of the waterside.

> *Farewell Bridge Foot and Bear* thereby,*
> *And those bald pates that stand so high.*
> *We wish it from our very souls,*
> *That other heads were on those poles.*

Without membership of the guildhalls, inns were the most suitable public places to do business, since such matters could not be discussed in church. The riverside was a place to spot traders selling exotic and incredibly expensive goods such as perfumed oil and spices. There were Italian and Spanish bankers, Jewish moneylenders and merchants from Norway to Russia. London was the starting point for most people entering the county. It was also where British citizens went to resolve legal problems, to hire lawyers and accountants, and to

---

* Names of local inns in the area – now demolished.

visit doctors and other professionals such as specialist tailors and printers.

The River Thames was at the heart of all this activity, and the lifeblood of Britain's capital. The author of the *Polychronicon*, Ranulph Higden, writing in the 1300s, described the special nature of London and its waterways. He illustrated how it was possible to sail a craft from Dorchester, in Oxfordshire, to the sea, using natural waterways. The route was used for taking things out as well as bringing them in. There were fortresses and strong walls with gates, by which the comings and goings of the populace, as well as the produce on which the economy was built, could be checked, and, more importantly, taxed.

Since the river was such an important aspect of the economic foundation of the city, its bridges were points at which trade could be monitored and controlled as well as tolls levied against those hoping to sell inside the city walls. The medieval world operated various systems of tolls and charges. There were tolls to pass over lands, tolls to trade in shops or from a tray in the street, tolls to sell goods on land owned by the church ... The list was extensive, and also covered the use of waterways. Most could expect to pay a fee to travel on or across water, unless it was a 'free river' like the Severn. Arriving in London and planning to pass London Bridge, you could be charged *wharfage* or *pontage* and eventually *doortoll* or *hucktoll* to sell the goods. There was *stallage* for hiring a pitch to sell from, and *cartage* for the hire of a wagon to transfer the goods along the road. It is small wonder that there were regular complaints about aldermen and city burgesses trying to screw every penny out of tradesmen. It also explains the general delight in stories about greedy tax collectors and the heroic criminal figures who outwit them in tales, such as Robin Hood.

The water provided more than a source of revenue. Fishing weirs could be installed along a river at various points to divert fast-flowing water to operate wheels for fulling stocks, to process cloth or grind corn. Those who ran or leased such concerns were themselves often extremely unpopular figures for their abuses of the system. Individuals paying for the use of the mill were being charged by deduction of weight as a percentage. Bearing in mind that in the Middle Ages it was illegal to grind your own grain and to possess a grindstone, many families who couldn't afford to lose the miller's cut were forced to process flour illegally.

Constructed weirs allowed a more industrial approach to accessing a food source. Fish could be pushed by an inverted obstacle towards a point in the river where conical traps called garths or putcheons would be laid. It meant that quantities of fish could be caught at once and, more importantly, kept alive for longer until they could be harvested. These traps were supposed to be authorized, but, where permission was not given and food was scarce, locals would install them anyway. Shallow-keeled boats were easily obstructed by them. Meanwhile, the riverbank's growing population was putting more pressure on the natural waterways, and it was increasingly difficult to navigate the tributaries to and from the Thames. Soon, the capital's waterways were going to have to be engineered by man.

Building a bridge often involved creating a practical ford to move animals, or diverting the natural run of the water until the work was finished. Fords, especially if broad, often meant that water levels were not high enough for a craft to pass, especially in a period of drought. Bridges could create the opposite problem. A poorly constructed bridge in waterlogged ground might easily collapse when faced with heavy traffic. If this happened, it was a very difficult task to remove the large pieces of masonry from the waterway. A town's future might rely on its ability to solve a problem such as this.

London's famous bridge, seen from seventeenth-century engravings as a ramshackle and dangerously overdeveloped route into London, had so many supports to hold it up that it created a type of undershot force in the fast-flowing currents between pillars through each of its 20 arches. This was hardly helped by the high water levels passing the bridge. For safety's sake it was advisable for passengers to get out and allow an experienced boatman to 'shoot' the craft through, sometimes with a lightened load for fear of overturning. The engineering solution of holding a bridge up by the suspension method was yet to be invented, so arches tended to be squat. The current when the tide was high or after sustained rains meant that craft might have to moor up for long periods, being unable to pass the bridge. In such cases it was usually cheaper to pay up for haulage rather than wait and risk goods being spoiled, stolen and excessively taxed.

> *London Bridge is falling down, falling down,*
>   *falling down.*
> *London Bridge is falling down,*
> *My fair Lady.*
>
> *Build it up with mud and clay, mud and clay,*
>   *mud and clay.*
> *Build it up with mud and clay,*
> *My fair Lady.*

The famous rhyme was based on a number of collapses and partial falls before the fifteenth century. Londoners might have realized that tolls demanded of them were necessary for maintenance but still complained when they were raised, and especially if they didn't believe the funds were being put to good use. The collapse of London Bridge in 1281 was widely blamed on the unpopular Queen Leonora of Castile – the 'fair Lady' and first wife of Edward I. It was under her name that revenues were generated, and the nearby monument Charing Cross was erected for her after her death.

The end of Plantagenet rule in England after the death of Richard III saw a population explosion and the growth of the middle classes. By this time, the upper reaches of the bridge extended well over the river itself. In the event of fire, dwellers were forced to leap into the water – the bridge had been so extensively built upon that they were trapped on all other sides. Rapid building had the effect of making the original twelfth-century crossing – with space enough for two carts – now half the width at just four feet. Traders and their wagons had to take turns to cross and, despite paying the tolls, could be waiting for hours. The frenetic pace and the impatience to get through to secure a good market spot often led to fights and injuries. Passers-by could be trapped between carts or crushed against buildings, injured by falling goods from the back of wagons or by animals herded or ridden over the bridge. Drowning was also common as many inexperienced visitors were prepared to take a chance to navigate the water themselves, or put their trust in ferry men along the banks. It was not until the rebuilding of the bridge by John Rennie in 1831 that citizens saw the back of the medieval bridge commissioned by Henry II.

This view of London in the 1670s shows the extent to which London's population and its boundaries had spread. The need to demolish the haphazard structures that had sprung up either side of the water had become increasingly evident.

After the Great Fire of London in 1666, the architect Sir Christopher Wren presented Charles II with plans to rebuild the city and do away with riverside overcrowding, but the authorities soon found that demand on the waterside was so great that new dwellings sprang up again almost immediately. London's other river systems had to take the strain, and engineering solutions began to be explored to make them work to better advantage. There were a number of developments along the banks of the Thames in the late 1700s and early 1800s to provide better facilities and access to them. This would be partly achieved in the building of modern docks situated away from the river along canal cuts, such as the one leading to the West India Dock, engineered by William Jessop and Ralph Walker, which opened in 1802. This was in the relatively rural borough of Poplar, opposite Greenwich on the river. The wet dock was made deep enough to admit ocean-going vessels and gave ample acreage for workers to load ships for export in what would be the foundation years of empire expansion for Britain.

The East India Dock followed beyond the Isle of Dogs in 1806 at the bend in the river known as Blackwall. The London Dock at Wapping had also been authorized by Parliament in 1800. From the outset, it was intended to be a heavily populated area and involved the forced demolition and displacement of thousands of households. By this time, London could boast a number of new bridges and developments such as St Katharine Docks, close by the Tower of London, designed by Thomas Telford and built in 1824. What Wren and King Charles had not been able to do following disaster and crisis, money – and the opportunity to make it – was to do for them more than a century later.

EARLY NAVIGATIONS

The River Fleet, the capital's second river, was important enough to be legislated for and used to generate income for the Crown. In 1110, the building of St Paul's new cathedral was reliant on the Fleet for the provision of the stone which would form the new Norman church after the earlier one had been destroyed by a fire in 1087, shortly after the completion of the record of assets and accounts later known as Domesday Book. Under Norman administration, tolls were imposed along this and other London waterways for the wharfage of craft, generating a fund for maintenance. The navigation was prone to problems with silting and slippage in the banks; this would be a long-term problem due to the tidal nature of the Thames, increased traffic and the erosion caused by repeated building and repair of quays. Common complaints in the period of increased global trade of the 1500s concerned the width and depth of the river and the lack of work to maintain it for the passage of craft. On the Thames, work was regularly ordered to dredge and ballast to keep smaller tributaries clear, but this largely depended on investment from wealthy citizens who wanted to keep trading.

Bye-laws covering the care of a waterway or a roadway could be very specific in preventing the fouling or obstruction of a transport network. Local courts and guilds were regularly troubled with complaints against those who failed to keep to the rules, or who knowingly polluted the rivers. This was especially important given the population's reliance on them not just for drinking water but for the operation of the cottage industries that formed the backbone of the local economy. Particular offenders were the officials who were supposed to be responsible for cleaning up the streets and looking after the sewerage of private houses. These were known as gongfermours or gong (dung) farmers. Their role was to empty latrine pits and sell waste to landowners outside the city walls, who could use it as manure for crops. Not all of the waste could be disposed of in this way, especially in areas where soil quality was good, so anything which couldn't turn a profit had to be dumped.

Because the Fleet was a smaller waterway, it was polluted more quickly. By 1652, the problem had become so intense that complaints from the guildhall and officers of the county of Middlesex forced the Mayor to take action. The British

Museum holds the original petition for sewerage cleansing and rebuilding of infrastructure around the Fleet Bridge.

Royal councillors in a planning meeting in 1667, following the Great Fire of London, recommended that a new bridge be built with greater passing space underneath. They proposed to make the river more navigable by cutting a deep channel and providing sluicing locks. They also discussed imposing new tolls once the work was done, which would then pay for continued repair work. There would be watchmen to enforce payment of the tolls and to prevent craft using the dock before the work had been completed.

The creation of a man-made canal on the Fleet was suggested by Sir Christopher Wren and Robert Hooke, the surveyor of buildings and rebuilding for the city of London. Their suggestion was taken up by the city aldermen but the work was difficult to complete because of obstructions, problems shoring up the wharves and regular assaults and attacks on the 200 contractors by lightermen and bargees. The work soon fell behind schedule and, as the aldermen discovered upon inspection, not even built to their specifications. The plans were changed to include the construction of a boom at Fleet Ditch to stop illegal users from entering and disturbing the works. Wren recommended that the ditch be shored up with brick and stone instead of timbers. The project cost the city nearly £50,000, an enormous amount, but which covered the maintenance of the channel as well as its construction. The aldermen were pleased enough with Wren's suggestions and oversight of the project, while rebuilding the city and working on St Paul's Cathedral, to award him a bonus of 190 guineas in 1673.

When the Fleet navigation was completed and opened in 1675, it ran from the Thames past both Bridewell and the Fleet debtors' prison, under two bridges and terminating into the brook at Holborn. Even though the first weeks saw good trade, there were still problems with silting and damage to the wharves from use of heavy carts and horses. Tolls were poor and collected in a disorganized manner. In the early 1700s, the project was acknowledged a failure, and contracts were made by the city to fill in and pave the cut between the bridges and eventually to cover the entire line to assist in the building of the Blackfriars Bridge in 1760.

Although this early waterway was at the end of its life, new canal schemes were now being proposed and petitioned for in Parliament. One success was the navigation of the equally ancient River Lea, upon which the people of London had the right to travel free of tolls, though tolls were charged against goods at weirs and locks. This route served Hackney Down to Bow Bridge and the Limehouse cut at the point the flow became tidal. And wherever there were sites of 'advantage' and mooring for vessels along theses tributaries, there was opportunity …

SPECULATORS AND INVESTORS

A small agricultural community based around an area like Clapham could take advantage of being along a major waterway, and, as the value of the land and proximity to London increased, so would its population.

The problem with this was that, while some villages were along natural creeks and courses, it was mainly a matter of luck. If businessmen wanted to take advantage of the nearby Thames, it meant cutting in and creating a waterway, a canal, as opposed to a simple navigation. This would require investment beyond what one man could provide.

There were canal systems on the Continent which, leading up to the eighteenth century, had been widely praised for their facility in transporting food and fuel in bulk to population centres. Until the mid-eighteenth century, there was little incentive for London to follow suit; trade coming in from the sea was enough.

By the middle of the century, however, it was a different story. In addition to the growth of the capital, former small towns were rapidly becoming seething metropolises, and 1700s society was very different from that of Tudor England. Trade had expanded overseas, with chartered companies setting up trade agreements in Africa, India and China, as well as the colonies in America and Australia. Higher demand for manufactured goods forced industrial production to gear up. As a result, the numbers of people looking for work or a better life in the capital exploded.

After centuries of the population being decimated by plague, the numbers were on the rise. By the 1600s, the whole country's population was around 5.5 million. What is more, population levels continued to grow because death rates were slowing. Aside from a spate of alcohol-related deaths (specifically gin) in the 1730s and 1740s, fewer deaths were being recorded, and this proved to be a continuing trend. Making a living from farming was becoming harder, even before the Agricultural Revolution and the land enclosures, and city life was attracting increasing numbers. Not only was the capital swallowing up immigrants from Europe, but Irish, Scottish and English rural labourers were coming in droves. While only adding around 8000 new residents per year, for London's eighteenth-century infrastructure it was like trying to put residents up in a small caravan park at the rate of a few hundred extra a week.

It wasn't just the poor arriving, either. It had become fashion-able, as the boundaries of London spread, to rent or build a town residence. If lords and ladies came to London, at least for part of the year, so would their lawyers, agents, servants and friends. Following them would be the middle classes and the self-made men, eager to mix in the right circles. All of these people needed goods and services, so more newcomers appeared: clergy, undertakers, accountants, smiths, grocers, shoemakers, tailors, clock and cabinet makers, dancing masters, grooms, coachmen, messengers, painters, plus, of course, prostitutes, quack doctors, thieves and thief-takers. More people than ever before now had access to a form of education and some degree of literacy, thanks to the availability of printed texts in English, and there was a greater chance to hear and debate news. General standards of living were improving, and the middle classes had grown. In fact, by the turn of the nineteenth century, London's population had doubled to 1,117,000.

The make-up of the city was so varied, and it was growing so fast, that the metropolis created an environment where a person might be able to find opportunities unavailable elsewhere. Those who did so lent a culture of capitalism and free market to London before the term was even created. Not all the new citizens were able to do so. Some carved out their niches and thrived in a competitive market; others found that, faced with the harsh reality of sink or swim, they sank.

Keeping the residents fed and watered was one of the biggest challenges, and only possible because of links to large arable farms in Essex and Kent. With limited supplies arriving slowly by a combination of river and road routes, it meant that prices would remain high and people were more likely to be palmed off with poor-quality goods.

It wasn't just food that was needed. As London expanded and spread to swallow up outlying villages to the north and south, the waterways also needed to link up to provide access to raw materials and manufactured goods only available further up country. Building materials were needed, too. For these, local rivers and small canal cuts would not be enough. London needed a long-haul trunk route to the new centres of industry. Creating these transport networks and making them work would depend on major investment and organization, which would be impossible without legislation and willingness to speculate.

From the medieval to the early modern period, the city had been dominated by the guilds and worshipful livery companies. Access to jobs for craftsmen was controlled by membership of one of these bodies, which required a subscription fee. This permitted them to operate in the city limits and provided customers with a feeling of confidence that there would be regulation of the trade. Companies provided livery coats, which made it easy to recognize who was 'in', and they had charitable arms in the community to do good works. Getting into the guild could be tricky and would involve serving out a seven-year apprenticeship to a guild master under low wages and strict regulation, but was often worth it to be made a 'free man'. Once made a 'journeyman' and having paid up, you could open a business and even pass it to a son, and in some cases a wife or daughter. The downside was that because the guild acted like a protector and made sure its members could work, its monopoly could only be safe if the number of guilds men was limited. So even serving an apprenticeship might not secure you a place. There are songs and stories of the apprentice, thrown out by the master just short of the term, or the apprentice finding that, at the end, he cannot pay into the guild.

> *When I was bound apprentice, in famous Lincolnshire,*
> *full well*
> *I served me marster, for more than seven year.*
> *Then I took up to poaching, as you will plainly hear,*
> *Oh tis my delight on a shiny night, in the season of*
> *the year.*

('The Lincolnshire Poacher', English folk song)

The guilds continued to be influential and sponsored schools and charities to support the trading establishment. But in the 1750s London City Council wanted to get the city to work at the pace needed to keep up with expansion of markets and overseas trade. The council decided to curb the monopolies, calling for non-liveried men to be hired as part of a freer market. Gradually, the guild dominance in economic terms was reduced until the companies which remained had a mainly charitable and social function. The relaxation of the economic order meant that more entrepreneurial characters could operate within the City of London and in the new towns free from restrictions altogether.

The same principles began to be applied to the chartered trading companies which had previously been under royal or state licence to operate in particular regions for the trading of British goods for exotic crops like coffee, sugar and tobacco, so readily consumed by the surging city. In the seventeenth century these companies had also had monopolies and their profit margins were very high, making them wealthy and influential. Their influence declined with depression in traditional trades in the pre-industrial period as well as a difficulty in obtaining enough goods cheaply. Gradually, the companies began to be diluted with larger memberships in order to stay in business, and covered risk by allowing the purchasing of shares in joint stock organization.

The first to be founded solely on this basis was the East India Company. The venture was so successful, and popular, that other companies followed suit at a time when cultural response to speculation was changing and one man's shilling (or guinea) was as good as another's. It was a lot less risky to own shares in a big, government-backed company than to put all your eggs in one basket with one independent vessel and captain. At least if a ship sank it was not the only ship, and there was less likelihood that an investor would lose everything.

It was a more flexible market, but still not a free one. Government intervened, not only with the passing of canal and navigation acts, but also with other protective measures. After periods of poor wool trading in the 1600s, navigation acts were passed and statutes put in place to prevent unfinished wool broadcloth being exported, and that which was exported had to be in a majority of English ships. Apart from strengthening the waterways, this had the effect of boosting the shipbuilding trade and the merchant navy at the same time. All of the prosperous docks and companies trading in the new colonies were based in London and brought in tremendous profits. This boom created more wealth and speculation, to such an extent that London, although mostly handling imports, had to allow exports to be handled at other ports. This spread the wealth and continued to develop infrastructure, based on the accessibility of water navigations to move raw product and to receive imported luxuries.

Ordinary people might now expect to have more than one set of clothing, and attempt to follow fashions more closely than they had before. They might go to the playhouse, buy broadsheets in the street and purchase prints and furnishings for their houses. Over the course of the next hundred years, cheap manufactured goods became more sophisticated and varied. As real wages rose, so did standards of living, meaning more 'spare money' in the economy.

All of this was made possible because individual engineers and craftsmen had come up with ways to make a process of manufacture cheaper, easier and faster. A scheme to build a factory or excavate for lead, copper and iron meant finding an investor. An entrepreneur had to come to the table with some of his own capital and show he was prepared to risk it on a well-planned venture. Doing so encouraged others to follow suit. But where was the table and who were the investors? The men who would put up the money could be those who already had a local or nationally recognized name, social standing and reputation. They also had to be prepared (and able) to wait for their money to show a profit, and survive if it didn't.

PUTTING CAPITALISM TO WORK

Many of the business deals and arrangements to loan and to further invest money were made in London's new chocolate and coffee houses, such as Lloyd's, Child and what would eventually become Barclays, all still in operation as banks. They were created and used by those who didn't, or couldn't, put the money into land and wanted it to grow. These were the days of speculation on a grand scale.

Banking was not the most reliable source of funds for development. Large banks were based in London, and the risk for those works setting up in the Midlands and the north in turning to independents seemed too great. Banks could, however, lend more confidently to other businessmen already engaged in trade who might in turn invest in infrastructure, even if it was not directly related to their main business. Investing surplus money was a wise move, because the interest owing on government approved bonds was kept stable and in turn kept the commercial market place afloat. The reliability of the Bank of England and the financial markets around London was reassuring for investors, who knew that their debts were unlikely to be called in quickly as would be the case if they borrowed from acquaintances or from smaller banking businesses. Investment through banks outside London was more dangerous because, apart from the risk of a few investments failing and dragging down the whole bank, there was an element of regional or local banking where, in remote areas, a monopoly on lending could occur. Landowners mortgaging their property for loans could be at risk of pressure from the bank to make decisions or deals which suited them.

If London banks couldn't be relied on and a local one was used, the added danger was that, should investments be unsuccessful, the bank might not be able to recoup the losses and might be unable to stay in business itself. To avoid the instability of banking collapses, the setting up of limited-liability, shareholder-run banks in the 1800s allowed big firms based in London to branch out into new economic centres like Manchester and Birmingham. Necessity drove expansion in the banking world, and the number of banks outside the capital doubled in the last 20 years of the eighteenth century as a result.

Established large banks in London traditionally secured investments connected to state-sponsored projects, which were less likely to fail. It was unlikely that a person's savings in the Bank of England would be wiped out through investments, but it also meant that returns were modest. Where there was little risk there would be a comparable amount of gain. London banking and speculation through the state was not a get-rich-quick scheme. But a lot of money could be made in a relatively short time by investing in those industrialists who were investors and shrewd businessmen, provided they could protect their patents and control competition. In an environment with few regulations to adhere to, no limits on hours worked, no provision for health and safety and no legislation on basic wage or conditions, overheads could be low and the market voracious.

By the late 1700s, companies could have hundreds of shareholders. Before the Industrial Revolution, investors were limited to a small group who had to agree to be financially responsible for the whole venture, not just their level of investment in it. That made businessmen wary because the failure of a factory might mean financial ruin. The key was to go in on as grand a scale as possible in order to be at the forefront of the market. If a business could supply better, faster and cheaper than anyone else, its goods would be in high demand and they could lead the market. Many companies fell foul of problems with equipment, transport, copying of machinery, underselling their goods or allowing too much credit. The most ruthless and determined characters were far more likely to be in a good state of business five years after starting up, by which time their shareholders could expect to start seeing revenues come in.

The cultural acceptance of consumerism provided a steady home market for British goods. But to have British goods you needed British sources of fuel and a means of transportation.

Small navigations and short canal cuts were financed by close associates, but major developments needed big money. As a result of changes to the law in the wake of the South Sea Bubble, that meant securing an Act of Parliament.

To drum up support for a canal scheme, a meeting would be announced and advertisements would go out in newspapers as well as invitation by letter to eminent men or landowners who might be affected. Mentioning the name of a respected businessman or engineer didn't hurt; neither did holding the meeting in a place favourably associated with business deals. The point of the meeting was to set out the business plan for a canal, give ideas of scope and cost and hear from engineers or senior investors. The presence of landowners gave townspeople and potential investors confidence and encouraged the word to spread.

Provided the Act was passed and the start-up costs could be raised quickly, the opportunity to make money 'for nothing' soon became apparent. This was the start of the boom years of canal construction, and there was a frenzy of public interest in the new investment opportunities on offer. There were fortunes to be made – and lost – from speculating on this new mode of transportation. Private capital had a role to play in driving the huge changes the country was experiencing. A new industrial society was being shaped by the investments of ordinary shareholders.

The efforts of the Duke of Bridgewater in creating a canal to bring coal mined on his estates to Manchester demonstrated that a willingness to invest and lead the way allowed him to capitalize on his holdings. The Bridgewater Canal was a speedy success, despite concerns that the planned aqueduct built by engineer James Brindley would not work. Others quickly followed suit.

THE MAKING OF THE NEW GRAND JUNCTION

At the height of this mania, one of the key English canal routes was given the go-ahead. The earliest, Limehouse Cut, from the Lea navigation had been authorized as early as 1766. The Grand Junction Canal, connecting London with Birmingham, via Warwick, Leamington Spa, Daventry, Northampton and Milton Keynes, began life as a number of different proposals. The Oxford Canal had proposed a link directly to London, and a route via Hampton Gay and Uxbridge from the Oxford was also put forward. A London to Birmingham line was extremely important because of the need for building and raw materials for the mercantile trades. London needed the coal, iron and bricks that the Midlands could provide but, by the early 1790s, there still wasn't a practicable way to do it. Supporters who wanted a quick route to London had seen that a canal from Oxford was popular because of its Thames link, but that there was a very great disadvantage: it was not fast because of the meandering course it followed. Investors felt that, even if major engineering was needed to create a line, it would be worth it for the distance and time saved.

The first meeting was held at the Crown and Anchor tavern on the Strand, in the heart of the City. The chairman was a Cornish banker, William Praed, who had headed up the campaign to have the Act passed and raise interest in its building.

Praed would eventually set up his own bank on Fleet Street in 1803, but at the time he was a senior partner in a London bank and had managed to acquire the support of the enormously wealthy Marquis of Buckingham, the Duke of Grafton, Earl Spencer and numerous other wealthy businessmen.

There was disagreement over the number of locks and the construction of tunnels, and over what route to take. The existing canal companies were keen to retain as much traffic as they could for their own routes to maximize tolls. The Oxford and the Thames and Severn canal companies put forward the London and Western ('Hampton Gay') canal scheme, running down to Isleworth, Middlesex. This proved impractical, because of problems with the water supply. A deal was eventually reached: a decision was made to build the Grand Junction between Brentford and Braunston, in Northamptonshire, while the Oxford Canal company would be paid up to £10,000 a year in compensation. Once these squabbles were sorted out, and the route decided on, the Grand Junction could apply for authorization through an Act of Parliament and start drumming up investors. This process began with an advertisement in a local paper.

Canals got most of their capital from local shareholders, from grandees down to the £50 shares of scores of innkeepers and widows. Moderately affluent people were now finding it more convenient to have their wealth in securely invested capital than in pockets of land. In 1792, a meeting at an inn in Stoney Stratford, a village near Milton Keynes, attracted so many would-be subscribers that they had to move to the parish church. The promoters were asking for £250,000, but a million pounds was promised there and then. Once a subscriber had his name on the list, it entitled him to shares, and he could begin trading these promised shares virtually immediately. The huge amount of interest in the Grand Junction soon generated a speculative bubble. Before the end of the year shares had quadrupled in value.

> At a sale of canal shares in October, 1792, ten shares in the Grand Junction Canal, of which not a sod was dug, sold for 355 guineas premium; a single share in the same canal for 29 guineas premium.
>
> (Baines, *The History of the Commerce and Town of Liverpool*, 1852)

And this was before the company had even started digging a canal or got approval from Parliament.

The Grand Junction received its Act in April 1793. With the initial investment in place, work could begin. First, though, there were more obstacles to overcome that would send costs spiralling upwards, putting potential profits for shareholders in jeopardy. Two local aristocrats, the Earls of Essex and Clarendon, both objected to the Grand Junction being routed through their lands. They had to be bought off: they were given shares in the canal and thousands of pounds for the purchase of the land, and the canal company had to build two elegant Gothic bridges on their lands. In addition, no boatmen were permitted to set foot on the Duke of Clarendon's land. The canal company also had to buy out mill owners at Tring, Aylesbury and Ivinghoe, who were concerned about vital water supplies being diverted.

The chair appointed James Barnes and, later, William Jessop as surveyors. Barnes, as chief engineer, was given the duty of arranging for all construction materials and the general works. He was to be paid 'For his services at the rate of two guineas per day, and half a guinea per day for his expenses'. This was an enormous amount, and Barnes was employed by the company for the next 12 years, which adds up to a large financial commitment to his expertise alone. Despite this, Jessop was kept on to oversee the construction. During the period before the canal was completely opened in 1805, a number of other eminent engineers, particularly experienced in canal building and in particular, geographical and physical problem solving, were also called in to give advice.

The line began to be cut from both ends at once. This was sensible because it meant that parts of the line could be used before the whole was completed, bringing in important revenues. Major engineering efforts would be the two main tunnels needed along the route, one at Braunston – a hub on the network, and in effect a crossroads where a link could be made to the Oxford Canal and to Leicester to the north – and the other tunnel at Blisworth in Northamptonshire, in the landholdings of the Duke of Grafton, one of the project's major supporters.

Work began almost immediately at Braunston. There were problems with the nature of the land: quicksand was discovered, and a mistake in the drafts for the work ended up producing a tunnel with an S-shaped bend. This made it more difficult to judge how to manoeuvre boats through it without their being damaged. Braunston became the place where boatmen would arrange for messages to be delivered, meet relatives and do business together. That made it a centre for smaller industries supplying the boat trade, as well as a magnet for religious and social interventions among the canal dwelling population.

There were problems at Blisworth, too. Construction difficulties were compounded by a serious accident which occurred during the work to break through the ironstone. Water flooded through from compromised walls. A series of other accidents involving machinery and falls of stone, as well as the discovery of quicksands, put the project back considerably. As if this wasn't bad enough, the siting of the tunnel was found to be unsatisfactory. Barnes called for a second opinion on its construction. The eminent engineer John Rennie advised that the diggings should be moved slightly to the west of the original line. Although this was essential, the work had to be delayed because of a shortage of money. When changes were put in place, they resulted in a shorter tunnel (although it remains the third longest in the network).

Apart from Blisworth, most of the canal was open for business by 1800. It knocked 60 miles off the previous meandering route via the Oxford Canal and was far more reliable. Now, finally, the canal could start earning money for its shareholders.

A boat's tonnage was estimated by a process called 'gauging', the measurement of the amount of water displaced when a boat was loaded with cargo. The toll was then calculated per ton per mile, and according to the types of goods being carried: lime and limestone at a farthing; livestock at half a penny; coal and coke at three-halfpence. Special rates applied when joining or leaving the Thames or Oxford Canal. Once it was up and running, the new canal thrived: in 1810 it carried nearly 350,000 tons of goods through London, with roughly equal amounts going into and out of the capital. This success led to another bubble. Share prices tripled in the 1810s. And, thanks to the London Stock Exchange being established in 1801, trading could now take place on a wider scale.

The success of the Grand Junction led to the building of extra branches, notably a connection from the Grand Junction main line at Southall to Paddington. Paddington was much closer to the heart of the capital and was served by the 'New Road' connecting it with the City. Parliamentary powers were quickly sought for this extension and the process of buying land and negotiating with difficult landowners began.

The Paddington arm from Southall to Camden was begun in 1794. According to the minutes of the Grand Junction Company:

> It is ordered therefore, that a survey be forthwith made by Mr Barnes, and inspected by Mr Jessop and that he report thereon to this committee as early as is convenient.

Convenient meant quickly and, even though the line was begun immediately, complaints flowed in. The work was progressing too slowly and the committee felt the resources were being mismanaged by chopping and changing crews from site to site. The shareholders were worried about finances, too, since the Paddington section had not been planned from the start of the project. Ideally, they wanted to raise a separate amount of money for Paddington to avoid falling short elsewhere and because, since tunnels had to be rerouted and repaired due to leaks and slippage, it was risky to rely on the existing capital. Barnes didn't appear to be in a hurry to answer the company's repeated questions about dates for completion, and by the winter of 1796 new shares had been floated to provide this extra cash flow and allow the engineers to get on with it.

Most canal schemes ran into opposition of some kind from those whose lands might be compromised or who were opponents of the spread of industrialization and tipping of the traditional balance of influence over communities. The line from Brentford to Paddington caused a certain amount of controversy, both in the route taken and the design along it. The Bishop of London's lands would have to be crossed. It became so difficult to deal with the Bishopric and there were so many arguments about how a route should be cut that a separate committee had to be appointed to deal with it. William Praed successfully concluded negotiations in 1798, allowing the completion of the final section to the basin and terminus.

> Mr White the Elder be requested to treat with Mr Crompton (landowner) and the Bishop of London upon any matter that may interfere with the general scheme in which their prospective properties or interests may be involved.

Mr White was responsible for the design of the bridge at Paddington. The committee took both stonemasons' and bricklayers' foremen to task over their 'deviation' from the plan and the resulting poor workmanship, which caused the bridge to be pulled down. This kind of costly mistake couldn't be allowed to be repeated and, from 1800 onwards, a higher level of scrutiny was applied to the remaining works, with more than 200 men employed full time to complete it. London was not joined directly to the national canal network until the Paddington arm of the Grand Junction Canal opened in 1801 (see Plate 1). The entire canal was eventually finished and opened in March 1805.

Fifteen years later, readers could buy the *Tour of the Grand Junction* by artist John Hassell. Partly because of the short-lived leasing of rights to run passenger packet-boat services out of Paddington Basin, he was able to travel the length of it, writing about and sketching the countryside north of London. Sixteen illustrations of the canal itself appear in his book and the impression is of the isolated nature of some of what would become the busiest points along the line, particularly at Stoke Bruerne and Braunston (see Plate 3). He noted that it was not only possible to see all of this landscape by boat, but that it was equally traversable on foot, via the canal's perfectly serviceable towpaths, should anyone choose to do so.

Rather more taken with the rural villages of England and points of interest away from the canal itself than with the industrial hotspots, Hassell couldn't fail to be impressed by the new basin at Paddington:

The basin at Paddington is a large square sheet of water occupying many acres, with warehouses on either of its sides, and so commodiously sheltered, that goods of every kind may be shipped or unloaded without the danger of being wetted.

(John Hassell, 1819)

The company reported around 342,000 tons of goods moved in 1810, with the majority being goods consumed by London. London's appetite was insatiable for Midlands fuel, iron, steel, bricks, York stone and woollens, cheap north-west textiles, Staffordshire's glass, ceramics and other factory-made domestic ware, and the market continued to expand. This was helped in great part by the building projects on the outskirts of London as the previously green fields of Islington, Hampstead, Camden and Hackney were covered over in seas of pavements, houses and shops.

Over 20 years, business continued in an optimistic fashion until the Grand Junction, along with its neighbouring canal lines, began to see a threat emerging in the shape of railways. There had been suggestions and attempts to amalgamate already, but they had come to nothing. In the 1840s, however, when it was clear that the railways would not be a passing fad, attempts to get the other canals to enter into talks about the future were made again, and the companies most affected agreed to talk terms. The main players – the Regent, Trent and Mersey, Coventry and Junction – met, along with some of the other northern lines, but the representatives of the Oxford and Warwickshire canals refused to come to terms. In the meantime, the Junction and its partners tried to compete for tonnage by reducing their tolls and speeding up transit as much as possible. The virtues of the steam engine had long been proven, and now experiments with steam to pump water and power boats was tried, but proved to be of little benefit in competition with rail.

The mid-1800s were troubled years for the company. A precedent was set when tolls were driven down to supply the railways with coal to free up the Great Western Railway and the London and North West Railway to take more passengers. A number of high-profile problems then occurred on the line, from complaints about steam tugs and the noise and damage they caused, to ones regarding reckless and endangering behaviour for which the company was held responsible.

> Complaints of repeated injuries to the works of the navigation (the linked Leicester Canal) of the steamboats belonging to the Grand Junction Co. And improper and reckless navigation of the Grand Junction Co. company steamers.

To try to make up for loss of trade with speed was inherently dangerous, and this was blamed for the accident to the barge *Wasp*, which took place at Blisworth Tunnel in 1861. When a steam-driven boat with another in tow entered the tunnel, they met with a pair of boats which were passing the traditional way, by 'legging it' through. Becoming entangled, the first boat passed but the craft it was towing became loose, preventing the other crewmen from escaping from the tunnel. They couldn't see because of the smoke generated by the engine, and were overcome quickly. The deaths by smoke inhalation and drowning which resulted included a man who had cadged a lift on the butty boat home to Stoke Bruerne. He was a carpenter named Edward Webb who had been working with the tunnel-repair team on a platform of wooden piles driven into the cut.

This and a famous explosion in 1874 at Regent's Park close to the Zoological Gardens encouraged the company to give up carrying. Instead, they allowed more to be done by the big carrying companies. The largest independent carrying company was Fellows, Morton and Clayton, who had taken over the traffic of the London-Midlands Carrying Company on the Grand Junction already. Although steam tugging was continued, the pressure was off the canal's shareholders and they were persuaded to try to create a monopoly by once again attempting to join up the whole regional network. Various schemes were put forward for the Junction to buy the Old Union canals and, in 1893, the company bought them for £10,500 and £6,500 respectively.

Having secured purchases, work began to widen and dredge the existing route to create better conditions for heavy barges. This was particularly important at Foxton on the Leicester branch of the canal, where wider boats would be able to increase the amounts shipped. The company now had access to coal in Derbyshire, and it was vital to get it out quickly and in bulk. That wasn't happening. The coal tonnage slipped down quickly towards 1900 and something drastic had to be done to improve Foxton Locks, near Market Harborough.

The building of an inclined plane seemed to be the answer. Two caissons were used in counterbalance with winch and wire ropes to draw a boat of 70 tons up the incline to and from the water levels without the use of locks. This method was much faster than sending two boats exchanging through the old locks, but was very expensive by comparison. The plane alone cost £40,000 and the cost of its steam operation was more than a pound per day.

Even in 1900, when the incline was open, its overheads were very high and, worse, Foxton and other improvements such as widening and rebuilding at Watford just didn't work. Coal duty, the company's principal source of income, continued to slump. The company was losing money hand over fist and

The Regent's Park explosion of 2 October 1874 was reported over a week later in the *London Illustrated News*. The article included graphic pictures of the destruction caused when the *Tilbury* ignited and blew up under Macclesfield Bridge on the Regent Canal with a mixture of gunpowder, petroleum and comestibles aboard. The boatmen died, but the bridge took the force of the blast and although houses were damaged, no other lives were lost.

The Foxton Inclined Plane was designed to speed up the process of getting a boat through the narrow and steep flight of locks there. It was only operational for a decade and closed in 1911 – this photograph dates from its last year of use.

couldn't continue. Eventually, the inclined plane was limited to daytime only, then abandoned altogether and sold as scrap in 1928. The remains of the tracks can still be seen at Foxton, passing alongside the older flight of locks, behind the brick-built boiler house where the steam winch was operated.

By the 1920s, the winding down of operations and the reductions in revenue meant that the Junction now looked to link with the remaining canal companies in the Regent and the Warwick. The Regent would only agree if the Warwick would come in, too. The firms had to consider the rapidly expanding road networks as well as the rail, and the only option was to band together in order to continue in operation.

Proposals were discussed in 1925 but it would be two more years before the holdings merged under a new name: the New Grand Union Company. The Junction acquired the Warwick and Birmingham Canal, and the new company ran the amalgamated business. The Grand Junction Company now managed the Paddington section and the basin alone. From now on, the Grand Junction was to be a property limited company only, meaning that it would be a landlord and that it would be subject to lower taxes, but that it would be more difficult to remove funds from it in future.

A new company running the main canal could issue new shares to raise money for more developments for wide vessels, as well as borrow £500,000 from the government to buy up existing branch lines. The Leicester and Loughborough canals were bought, as well as the Erewash.

Despite the attempt at investment, the grand expansion plan was never quite completed and the hope of universal widening along the line remained a pipe dream. The result was a time-consuming need to transfer loads to narrow boats at 'pinches' along the route and regularly cause enormous 'traffic jams' at pressure points. Nothing the company did helped. Their carrying company tried to develop the fleet and spent a great deal of money on new boats which were unable to turn a profit, and ended up being sold off to finance the debts.

Nevertheless, the story of canals as capitalist enterprises in a golden age begins here. With the Grand Junction, canal construction offered the capital a key route to industrialization. Those early improvements in transport and power allowed for a great leap forward in the scale of manufacture that pushed the development of the country to its zenith. The mass adoption (and affordability) of steam power and the development of machinery and processes to complement it turned a busy island into a global producer and superpower in the space of less than a hundred years.

2

THE ENGINEERS: YORKSHIRE

STILL CONSIDERED A SINGLE ENTITY, and the biggest 'old county' in the United Kingdom, Yorkshire makes up around one-eighth of Britain's land mass. Before the local authority amalgamations of the 1970s, most Yorkshire folk were used to the concept of the county as a whole, divided up into 'Ridings', based on geography. The earliest written records refer to the need to keep some sort of hold over what was essentially a wild frontier before the border with Scotland. Much of the land along the western boundary with Lancashire as well as the North Wolds was remote, rocky and inaccessible. As a result, it was poorly populated. In the fertile Dales and the south-eastern parts of the county abutting Lincolnshire, the farming was good and market towns developed thriving economies in the later medieval and Tudor periods as English trade began to expand.

The West Riding was initially one of the more problematic regions to adapt or profit from. Landlords here tended to have large holdings because the land produced less than further south; tenant farmers could pay only low rents on subsistence farming. The only way to make a profit was to engage in subsidiary crafts for sale.

The Domesday Book in 1086 describes much of the West Riding reaching from Calderdale to Skipton as 'waste'. That wasn't a description of the lands devastated in the northern rebellion against William the Conqueror; rather, it reflected their inability to make any profit for the manor lord. One use of land which would be more profitable than crop farming was sheep husbandry.

Common grazing for sheep formed the basis of the cottage industries around woollen and worsted production as well as hand knitting in later centuries in the Dales. This was a way for families to make a little extra money to pay their rents and have something to fall back on should harvests be poor, or sheep and cattle be taken by raiders from over the border. Gradually, as demand grew for these products outside of the local economy, landowners realized that it would be more profitable to farm sheep intensively in 'enclosed' fields. The 'crazy paving' of drystone walls which can be seen from above in this part of the world was begun in earnest in the medieval period by monastic houses such as Kirkstall Abbey in Leeds. The old ditch and bank boundaries used by villeins in small hillside communities were removed to resolve disputes over rights to access and accusations of trespass.

The lords of the manors followed suit. Some of them evicted free tenants from the land to raise large flocks of sheep, making themselves unpopular in the process. Further reliance on the wool industries would expand this system in the 1700s, while experimenting with breeding for bigger animals with different types of fleece.

During the Tudor age, changes were made to the types of farms which operated, as important landlords found it preferable to allow tenants to take over management of the land. This helped create a new class of 'middlemen', who would be partly responsible for creating a climate of stagnation in the cottage industry before the development of factories.

From the 1500s to the beginning of the eighteenth century, control of the industry for most of those engaged in turning wool into cloth was in the hands of the guilds and the middlemen. They determined how much to pay cottage weavers, depending on the prices finished goods would fetch. Merchants had to keep their outgoings low. The costly nature of this type of business meant that the people at the forefront of the trade were the first to lose out when export prices to principal buyers in Flanders, Germany and northern Italy were poor. Despite repeated attempts to control the wool trade and the taxes on it, demand remained high and even increased when British explorers began to establish trading posts in other continents. Bosses were free to determine prices and there was often great dissatisfaction among the communities of weavers, as one seventeenth-century ballad reveals:

Of all sorts of callings that in England be,
There is none that liveth so gallant as we.
Our trading maintains us to live as a Knight,
We live at our pleasure and taketh delight.
We heapeth our riches and treasure great store,
Which we get by griping and grinding the poor.
And this is the way we do fill up oour purse,
Although we do get it with many a curse.

('The Clothier's Delight; OR The rich man's joy, and the poor man's sorrow. Wherein is expres'd the craftiness and subtility of many Clothiers in England, by beating down their Work-Men's wages. Combers, Weavers and Spinners, for little gains, doth earn their money by taking of hard pains' by T. Lanfiere, British Library Roxburgh 4.35 Collection)

This part of Yorkshire was not the most productive sheep-farming area in the pre-industrial period, as most of the herds farmed were short-coated. Longer-coated breeds, most useful for spinning, were commonly found in the grassy fenland areas like Lincolnshire and Norfolk. Crossbreeding sheep to produce an animal with a longer coat, but which would do well on the hills, was an important step towards domination of the industry, but it would be the very nature of the hills themselves that made the difference when it came to mechanization.

The effect of this type of farming and the small pockets of industry that grew up alongside it resulted in a patchwork of fields and walls over rocky ground at high elevations above sea level. One traveller in 1777 described his journey through Derbyshire and Yorkshire as:

> Truly wild and romantic; nature here sits in solitary grandeur on the hills, which are lofty, green to the top, and rise in irregular heaps on all hands, in their primeval state of pasture, without the least appearance of a plough, or habitation for many miles.
>
> (William Bray, *Sketch of a Tour into Derbyshire and Yorkshire*, 1777)

The romance of the Pennine hills in the West Riding was inspiring for many, including the famous Brontë family, who lived further up-country on the moors of Haworth. But for the merchants, who needed to collect goods from farming communities to sell at market, the nature of the countryside was a trial. It was difficult for traders to travel around the districts with their 'pieces' for the local towns of Huddersfield, Halifax, Bradford or Leeds; it was even more trying for the long-distance merchants buying in bulk from the cloth centres. Taking goods to London or Liverpool for export was only possible by packhorse train to a port city and delivery around the coast. This meant traffic to Liverpool or to Hull. Leeds-born artist George Walker encountered people in remote areas as well as in towns and was particularly interested in how people went about their business. One of his coloured plates showed a packhorse team of cloth-makers heading for Leeds and Huddersfield and the 'piece halls':

> These men have a decided provincial character, and
> their galloways* also, which are always over loaded,
> have a manner of going, particularly their own.
>
> (George Walker, *The Costume of Yorkshire*, 1814, Yorkshire
> Archaeological Society, University Library of Leeds)

Another plate in the series shows a factory in a rural setting. Walker remarks on the child workers who were the subject of the sketch, noting that they were employed in making clothes which were needed by everyone, and would be fed, but it was at the expense of 'health and morals'.

Travelling by packhorse involved slinging sacks of cloth or pannier baskets over the backs of horses and travelling what were mostly primitive, uneven tracks. In poor weather, these

---

* Stout 14-hand ponies bred for travelling over uneven ground and long distance.

were often altogether impassable, and in some areas could be flooded, preventing horses from climbing ascents. Even in summer, high winds on the Pennines and moors made the going equally difficult. The temptation to overburden the animal must have been great, considering the expense of such a journey.

Passing from the village of Midgley across Luddenden Moor, for example, a distance of 19 miles, was the last leg of the journey from Burnley to the piece hall at Halifax. To make this journey along the packhorse trail, men would need to guard their train, buy food, feed and shelter their horses and dogs, as well as find somewhere to sleep. The cost of shoe leather alone over repeated journeys would have added a significant cost to the endeavour! A rhyme about the weavers' convoys from the late 1700s gives advice about walking the 'long causeway' and suggests that it is a brave soul who makes the journey all the way from north Lancashire to Halifax. The village of Marsden was another link between Lancashire and Yorkshire from Rochdale to Huddersfield. The modern road to Marsden passes over moorland which horses once travelled in numbers of up to 50 at a time, and the deep drops and steep hills are now popular with leisure hikers.

Although the wool stapling towns in the area were growing by the 1700s, they were still not considered cities. Leeds had the biggest population in the region as an established centre for trade, but as John Leland had described in the sixteenth century, there were numerous 'quik' towns locally which had developed wool textile specialisms and wanted to encourage growth. If you wanted to be at the centre of the trade in 1750, you would have had to travel to Norwich.

The many innovations of spinning, and later weaving, cotton and wool, would transform the fortunes of Lancashire and Yorkshire in the late 1700s. Towns where factories were built became dense centres of investment to which more people came to earn a steady wage, and hope for a better life.

The first factories arose from the installation of a number of spinning frames under one roof, powered by water. Water power had been used to great effect in the processing of numerous materials, from grain to wool, for centuries. Wool was cleansed and thickened in fulling mills positioned on fast-flowing water sources: the water turned a wheel which would 'paddle' wool and scour it, removing dirt and grease, in bulk before it was turned into yarn and woven into cloth. Waterwheels had been in use from the thirteenth century, but it had taken centuries for textile machinery to catch up. Once financiers put their weight behind innovations, spinning frames, looms and carding machines were built at a rapid rate. The levels of investment in the first mills were testament to the profits to be made. The inefficiencies and cost of the cottage

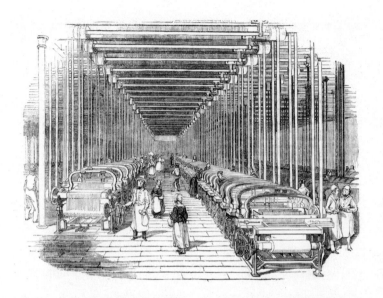

Edmund Cartwright's development of a stable power loom allowed
fully mechanized machines to be set up in large sheds to be run by
less skilled and fewer hands. Factory masters preferred cheap
labour and turnover in cities could be high.

system persuaded men with investment capital to build new
factories, as well as processing plants.

> A spirit of investigation is now prevalent, many of the
> cloth merchants have also become manufacturers,
> and have an opportunity of observing the effects
> of the hardness or softness of the wool producing
> on the cloth in a finished state ... The value of
> soft wool is better understood and it has greatly

increased. It may be affirmed that when taking two packs of sorted wool of the apparent same fineness, one possessing an eminent degree of soft quality, the other of the hard kind, the former will, with the same expense to the manufacturer, make a cloth, the value for which shall exceed the former by fully twenty-five per cent.

(Robert Bakewell, *Observations on the Influence of Soil and Climate upon Wool*, 1808)

In a handful of years, as one or two factories became 10, then 50, the old cloth market towns experienced a boom in business and population which most of them found difficult to cope with. When the Halifax gentlewoman Anne Lister visited nearby Bradford in 1825 to attend a court case, she heard about the troubles in the town over striking workers and intimidation. She mentioned a number of incidents of 'sad riots' in both West Yorkshire and Lancashire and tales of men 'pulling down power looms'.

Spinning frames had been tolerated to an extent in the district because they replaced work traditionally done by women. In the cottage environment more than one spinning wheel at work could supply enough yarn for one weaver's handloom and work could be picked up and put down as needed. Some 'combinations' or weavers' clubs encouraged people to work together where labour was intensive, such as in cropping or tentering to finish cloth, but real resistance to factories came when the skilled work of men was threatened.

The men responsible for such acts were known as 'Luddites', after a fictional leader called Ned Ludd, who appeared in pamphlets protesting about reductions in wages and the introduction of machinery in Nottingham, Derbyshire and Yorkshire and Lancashire's textile towns. Rising food prices and disruption in the markets had caused tempers to run high, and this culminated in 'cells' of individuals attacking machines and works in protest. Most damage to property and 'machine breaking' was done under cover of night or in disguise and it proved very difficult to prosecute offenders.

The Luddite response was relatively short-lived. With so many workers removed from their tight-knit communities and tied to the routine of factory hours and wages, resistance became less pronounced. Extreme actions such as mill burning and personal attacks discouraged many from getting involved, and the presence of large numbers of volunteer soldiers and dragoons also served to keep protests in check.

In a matter of 50 years, the previously small market town of Bradford (which 'stondith by clothying' when Leland had visited in the 1500s) had grown beyond its old medieval boundaries. A proliferation of textile mills in the centre of town had grown the population by 60 per cent according to

Luddites were commented on in newspapers and broadsheets for attacking the machinery that threatened their livelihoods, although they rarely did so in public view. Those most likely to act against mechanization were younger men, who would be the first to be out of work in competition with the factory system.

records made when the town was granted borough status in 1847 – though such records underestimated the true population because of the tendency for busy centres to absorb itinerants and temporary residents. Previously small places began to grow to such an extent that they outstripped formerly significant trading hot spots. Huddersfield jumped ahead of Halifax, because more new machines were taken there in the early 1800s than anywhere else in the region. As a direct result of textile expansion, Huddersfield became a centre for engineering and developed specialisms in industrial chemistry.

Acts of Parliament soon allowed the building of turnpike toll roads to link up businesses and move goods. But carriage in bulk by horse wagons was not much more efficient than the simple packhorse train, and the use of carriage by road was limited mostly to the mail and human cargo travelling from place to place. Such conveyances were not cheap, and could hold only limited numbers of people. The sheer scale of mass production meant that roads were unable to cope. The towns of Halifax, Huddersfield, Bradford and Leeds as well as Wakefield were all joined by turnpike roads, but that was not sufficient to meet demands. Water had been used to power the early mills, and now it would be adapted over land to deliver the goods, too.

Leeds already had dock areas along the Aire and waterside warehouses in which to store and sell goods. The Calder and Hebble was adapted so that it could serve as a link between

'CleckHuddersfax' (Cleckheaton, Huddersfield and Halifax) and Lancashire. Influential men on both sides of the Pennine border believed that if only the waterways could be expanded to take goods not just between convenient points on the local rivers but beyond, they would be able to receive raw products and fuels cheaply and fast, and get their finished goods to the consumer. Two canals were purpose-built to serve the area: the Leeds and Liverpool (with branches to Preston and Leigh) and the Huddersfield Narrow Canal, both still in use today. They were the result of entrepreneurial endeavour and they required a 'new breed' of civil engineers to solve the problems presented by the unforgiving terrain of the Pennines.

'THE FATHER OF CANALS'

The first famous name associated with the 'mastering of nature' for commerce was James Brindley. The eldest of seven children, Brindley was born in Wormhill parish near Tunstead in Derbyshire, and was recorded by his early biographers as being an unpromising young man. He was apprenticed at 17 to a local millwright, Abraham Bennett of Sutton in Macclesfield, who called him a 'blundering blockhead'. There are a number of references to young James being left in charge of the workshop and making a mess of repairs while trying out the skills he was learning. But he would soon prove himself a born engineer. One story had Bennett viewing a waterwheel and trying to copy it for a new paper mill on the River Dene. Passers-by questioned the sense of the model, and Brindley went to the mill to see how the idea could be adapted to suit its precise situation. Being practically illiterate, 'he could not make any notes', so out of necessity 'stored up all the particulars carefully in his head'.

This was one of many such anecdotes related by Samuel Smiles in his biography of Brindley in 1874, as part of his popular series *The Lives of the Engineers*. Smiles was particularly effusive about Brindley; 'the Father of Canals' represented the pinnacle of his world view. Here was a man who seemed to have raised himself out of poverty and ignorance to achieve wealth and fame by sheer ingenuity and hard work. He describes Brindley's father as a drunkard and a time waster, unable to provide for his family, which resulted in young James having to go to work as a farm labourer. Smiles based his work on a memoir of Brindley by Hugh Henshall, Brindley's friend and brother-in-law, as well as a fellow engineer. Henshall (unlike Smiles) knew Brindley's circumstances and even he described James's father as living a life of 'rural dissipation', which to the Georgian mind meant anything from laziness to hunting with dogs, attending cockfights and baiting and gambling. Such pursuits were not available to the poor cottage labourer, and details of the family's land suggest that, while not rich, Brindley's family were not without property.

The fact that Brindley was apprenticed was not unusual for the time but, as his father was a freeholder, his contemporaries were astonished that he should have had such a poor education. The son of a man of property would usually have expected to receive schooling privately, provided his father's estate drew profit. This does not appear to have been the case, as Brindley was unable to read and write well, although able to understand how things worked and to think in a logical way to solve problems. Being apprenticed to a millwright meant making working models before building equipment, pumps and wheels for industry. Brindley quickly acquired a reputation for reliable work among the silk workshop owners of Macclesfield, and those who required drainage works on their land. Having repaired a number of waterwheels, Brindley went on to build them for mill owners. He also gained experience in planning and digging tunnels in order to achieve the best levels of water for operation.

He eventually went into business for himself, moving to Leek in Staffordshire where his skills in mechanical engineering and problem-solving in the physical environment were put to good use. By 1776, he had come to the notice of the third Duke of Bridgewater, who was trying to find a way to create a waterway from the coal mines on his estate at Worsley to nearby Manchester. *Weale's Quarterly Papers on Engineering* records the meeting of the Duke and Brindley, and the demonstration of how a river breach could be repaired by 'agitating earth in a frame of water' to puddle it into a lining layer. The Duke was younger than Brindley and, while noted for his quick and energetic mind, like Brindley he was lacking in formal education. The Duke had found a man of ideas and practicality who he would be able to work with to get his canal built.

In building the Bridgewater Canal, Brindley lined it with stone and puddled clay to prevent leaking. Contemporaries scorned his methods, in particular the 'madness and folly' of the massive stone Barton Aqueduct (see Plate 4) to carry boats over the existing River Irwell at the point where Manchester and Salford meet. But the success of the cutting in bringing coal to a city growing fast on the profits of cotton made other industrialists sit up and take notice. Brindley was soon in demand as a consultant on numerous projects, one of which was the Leeds and Liverpool Canal.

THE LEEDS AND LIVERPOOL

It had begun life as an idea to improve the Douglas and Ribble waterways for carriage of goods between Manchester and the Lancashire towns of Preston and Blackburn in the early eighteenth century. Nothing came of the original plans, partly because of the economic crash of 1720; the South Sea Bubble made investors wary of throwing money and reputation after potentially ruinous schemes. But the rapid population growth and industrial expansion of the later 1700s gave transport projects more urgency, and the Bridgewater Canal's critics had been proved wrong. This prompted a number of Yorkshire businessmen to think of preparing a route to provide alternatives to overland movement of goods.

Although the canal is called the *Leeds* and Liverpool, the Yorkshiremen involved in pushing the Act through Parliament and gathering support had most of their business interests in Bradford. The character of the town was different from Leeds in that the lack of regulation and enforcement on building and commerce here gave it a 'frontier town' quality. Dominated by neither monopoly nor town council regulations, business might come to Bradford, but only if there was enough inducement to do so. In such an environment, keeping costs down helped a core group of innovators take advantage of the times and make their fortunes.

A Bradford businessman, John Stanhope, sent a Halifax engineer named John Longbotham to see for himself. Long-botham reported back that the proposals put forward by former businessmen in Liverpool to make a canal to cut the Pennines sounded plausible. John Hustler of Bradford later wrote that he was approached by Longbotham about a survey of the land reaching from Liverpool and Manchester to Hull. The route would pass through the Lancashire towns of Colne and Burnley (with a branch to Preston and Wigan), before joining the West Yorkshire towns of Bradford, Keighley and Leeds and then accessing Hull via the Aire and Calder navigation. Hustler and Stanhope had already been campaigning for a canal to ease the cost of bringing coal and limestone to Bradford. The two men were among the trustees of the Bradford Turnpike and, even though this had been designed to create revenues which would help their business and carriage, land transport continued to be too expensive. The Bradford contingent proposed two separate committees, one meeting in Lancashire and the other in Yorkshire.

In 1774, the men who were working to get the Leeds and Liverpool built had also raised funds for and built a small canal from the Broadstones area of Bradford, using water diverted from the Bradford Beck. In 1776, an initial meeting of the Yorkshire contingent was held at the Sun Inn in Bradford to discuss the results of Longbotham's first survey. He had planned a route from Liverpool to Leeds which skirted beneath some of the towns in north Lancashire, with cuts through from river navigations only possible by purchasing the River Douglas. The alternative was a more direct route to Liverpool, which would be easier (and therefore cheaper) to dig. The Lancashire committee, meeting in Liverpool, was not satisfied with this, however, and began to question the benefits of the scheme. They asked James Brindley to report on the findings of the survey and even employed more Lancashire-based surveyors to come up with an alternative route.

Yorkshire and Lancashire continued to quarrel over practicality and cost. Liverpool wanted the canal to run through Wigan and Leigh so coal could be brought to Liverpool without taking it by the coastal route, and Bradford wanted to supply the northern part of the region with its coal as well as bring stone and lime from the northern section. Under Lancashire's plans, the canal would be 20 miles longer and much more expensive. In the minute book for the Leeds and Liverpool, an instruction was given on 14 June 1769 for Longbotham to attend Brindley in Liverpool, bringing a letter of concern from the 'Gentlemen of Yorkshire' stating that they wanted him to settle things as the figure of authority and ensure that the Lancashire surveys had been properly carried out.

They had not been properly carried out, and this gave Yorkshire the grounds to reject an adapted plan. It was felt on the east side of the Pennines that Yorkshiremen had coughed up far more readily for the cost of the surveys and the putting through of the bill, and the money from Lancashire didn't appear to be forthcoming. After a period of silence, and worry that their partners were getting cold feet, some of the Bradford men headed west to persuade doubters and come to an arrangement. Everything hung in the balance as two lines were proposed at a general meeting at the Black Bull Inn in Burnley. Longbotham's proposals for a canal 66 miles long to take in Wigan and Leigh as well as Colne in the north were accepted and the Yorkshire committee agreed a few weeks later that, if all the subscriptions could be gathered, work could begin at both ends of the canal as soon as a bill was passed. Stanhope's death in 1770 at the point of the passing of the Act put John Hustler in charge in Bradford. Although an office was opened in Liverpool, the majority of decisions were to be made in Yorkshire where the company's main office was established.

Brindley was appointed chief engineer, but he didn't remain with the canal for long despite being paid twice the amount Longbotham received. By this point, Brindley's health was failing as he had been found to have Diabetes Mellitus (now commonly known as 'adult onset' or 'Type 2' diabetes). In 1767, Josiah Wedgwood's letters to his friend and business partner Thomas Bentley in Liverpool had described his concern for Brindley's health, complaining of him being so busily engaged by every scheme in the country that he was mentally and physically at breaking point:

> The great, the fortunate, money getting Brindley,
> an object of pity! And a real sufferer for the good of
> the Public. He may get a few thousands, but what
> does he give in exchange? His health, and I fear, his
> life too, unless he grows wiser, and takes the advice
> of his friends before it is too late.
>
> (Wedgwood Museum Archive)

It was too late for Brindley; he died in 1772 at the relatively young age of 55. It was left to Longbotham, the company clerk, to take on the job of chief engineer and oversee construction through some of the most difficult country.

After a number of difficulties and threats from competitive canals in Lancashire, the company secured the River Douglas, and the first section out of Liverpool was completed quickly. The going from Lady Walk in Liverpool was relatively easy, as was the Gargrave to Skipton, which involved skirting around moorland along natural contours, a method favoured by Brindley. Other areas of the route were more problematic for the company, and construction of tunnels on the Lancashire side of the route proved unavoidable. The sections which called for a more intensive engineering approach were to cost the company a considerable amount of time and money.

At Bingley, north of Bradford, there were two problems facing the canal builders. The first was how to cross the

This portrait of James Brindley, by JT Wedgwood, dates from the period after Brindley's death. He was greatly mourned by Josiah Wedgwood and had become well known and respected nationally for his expertise. The Barton Aqueduct sits behind him in the portrait as a representation of his legacy.

River Aire where at times of spate the waters thundered in raging torrents. At Dowley Gap, Brindley had designed an aqueduct with seven arches, spanning the Aire 30 feet below. The whole structure was built by navvies with only picks, shovels, buckets and wheelbarrows. It would be one of Brindley's last designs before he died. The second problem was getting the canal to 'rise' with the level of land as the line climbed to Skipton. Longbotham's solution was the famous 'five rise' locks, which were installed to take boats up by 18 metres to higher ground out of the 'bowl' of Bradford and into Wharfedale. This is the highest flight in operation on the longest stretch of canal in England, and it opened in March 1774 to great public excitement and acclaim. The *Leeds Intelligencer* described thousands of local people arriving to see the first boat rise through the locks. The reporter described all the locks and other features of the section including the Dowley Gap Aqueduct with its seven arches, which would be encountered after passing Shipley. He exclaimed that the 'joyful and much wished for event' was celebrated by loud music and ringing of church bells as well as the firing of muskets by the local militia.

There are two sets of rises on the canal at Bingley, the first in three stages, the next in five. The climb is sudden and steep and requires staff to live close by permanently in case of operation difficulties. The locks can only be successfully operated by setting all gates, so the role of lockkeeper is still an important one on this stretch of the canal.

This had been one of the more expensive sections of the works, and the committee was soon to discover that the £200,000 Brindley had suggested it would cost had already been spent. Hustler realized that there were miles yet to build, without funds. He complained that the wage bill alone was ruinously expensive. Stone was reasonably plentiful, but the cost of this as well as the works yet to be undertaken meant that more money would have to be raised.

This wasn't the only difficulty, as Longbotham was accused of a conflict of interest over his ownership of a coal mine and use of the canal to operate a packet-boat service. The committee wanted details about the expenditure on works he had supervised and found it difficult to bring him to account. Longbotham resigned in the summer, and the committee had to find another engineer.

The remaining stretch to conquer would be the Barrowford to Salterforth section, as the level drops into Lancashire. Here a tunnel would need to be dug at the summit of the hills at Foulridge, and more money had to be raised for it by another act of Parliament. The new engineer was Robert Whitworth, who in 1789 optimistically believed that the tunnel should not be particularly expensive or onerous compared to other tunnels. He was wrong on both counts. Work proved dangerous, slow and difficult – and it would be the most expensive part of the entire construction project.

The technique Whitworth employed for the tunnel became known as 'cut and cover'. It is still used today: a trench having been excavated and covered, an overhead support system is built over it then bricks are placed under the cover. The cover is removed and the excavated earth is piled on top of the bricks. Collapses were common, however, and when workers reached the central section of the tunnel, they found the rock so challenging they gave up on cut and cover. They were faced with laboriously boring through with picks and shovels. It took five years to complete.

In fact, the Leeds and Liverpool was taking so long to finish that other routes had been built in the meantime. The opening of the Rochdale Canal, work on which began two years before the Foulridge Tunnel was completed, worried some of the committee, who suggested that cutting such a tunnel could be avoided if the route was made to link other Lancashire towns that could not be served by the Rochdale. The alternative was to make the Leeds and Liverpool link up with other canals on the Lancashire side in order to bring stone from Skipton and Gargrave south. Confusion about the future of the Lancaster, Rochdale, and Manchester, Bolton and Bury all played a part in the final decisions about the route of the Leeds and Liverpool as deals were made, and criticisms levelled within the company as well as by the proprietors of rival lines. But profits were now coming in from the open sections of the canal, and dividends started to be paid, not least from the leasing of the Earl of Thanet's limestone quarries at Skipton, which proved particularly profitable.

By the time the Leeds and Liverpool was completed in 1816, its early supporters had all passed away. The canal linked with the Lancaster as well as the Bridgewater to Manchester via a junction from the Leigh branch, and flowed to Liverpool via the River Douglas. Even though the project was officially finished, there were difficulties with an adequate water supply for the Foulridge Tunnel. Leakage and poor maintenance led to demands for the route to be 'improved'. The tunnel could not be used at some points because of falling masonry, lack of water and silting on the banks, despite the cutting and deepening of the reservoir. At one stage, goods had to be carted over the top after the western end of the tunnel had collapsed. At times the whole of the Burnley section was unnavigable, and the rest of the canal was suffering from bursts and other repair issues. When the canal was fully opened, however, the profits began to roll in. Business from some Lancashire towns almost doubled until the 1820s. The increase in economic activity in the region would give rise to the establishing of entire new communities.

A COMPANY TOWN

The canal leading from Bradford towards Bingley and its famous locks is the home of Saltaire, probably the best known of the 'model' communities of the industrial period. By the time Titus Salt was ready to open his own works by the middle of the century, the canal was already well established. The son of a wool stapler, Salt had become very experienced in woollen and worsted textiles, working as a wool buyer and gradually buying up businesses in Bradford. His fame spread when Charles Dickens, writing in the popular family magazine *Household Words*, described Salt's 'discovery' of alpaca fibre in a Liverpool warehouse and how he began to experiment with working it under power. Alpaca and mohair proved to be runaway successes in the manufacturing of the fine dress fabrics for which he became well known.

With this initial success, the finances were available for Salt to purchase land by the canal and the Aire to build a 'vertical mill', or a factory where every part of the processing of cloth could take place. He chose this spot primarily for its position along the canal, where advantage could be taken of cheap carriage of fuel for his enormous factories and of easy access to water for processing in the scouring plant. The soft water flowing in the area was perfect for the conditioning of wool and fibres, and it was believed that the area, lying on the outskirts of industrial Bradford, offered the perfect combination of a semi-rural vista and proximity to an experienced labour pool. The turnpike road and the recently built railway also offered alternatives for transport and shipping products in and out.

Most firms in Bradford still operated by specializing in parts of the process, and putting out work to other firms, such as the finishing of woven cloth. Salt wanted autonomy; he aimed to create an independent borough along the Aire, not subject to the rule of Bradford or neighbouring Leeds.

Portrait of Sir Titus Salt, Baronet, MP for Bradford in 1859 and founder of Saltaire.

The continued expansion of Bradford as a borough and the control of Shipley (governed by its own council at the time) meant that he was not able to be lord of his own manor. Salt was much applauded during his lifetime, and afterwards, for the construction of a village which offered good-quality housing, as well as amenities designed to be improving for the workforce, the organizing of education classes, opportunities to attend chapel and bathhouse as well as play sports such as cricket (see Plate 6).

The ethos of the village was based on principles laid out in the work of Samuel Smiles reflecting Victorian cultural leanings toward 'industry as a way out of poverty' and the notion that a man could improve himself through the inspiration of success stories and magnificent surroundings. As a Nonconformist and supporter of temperance, Salt would not allow public houses to be built in the village and publicly stated that he believed drink to be the cause of all 'low behaviour and crime'. An 1850 report commissioned by Salt into the moral character of the town of Bradford lambasted the availability of alcohol and condemned most of the workers as unreliable, criminal drunks who could not improve their lives or their city.

Three miles away from the built-up and incredibly over-crowded city, the regulated and uniform layout of Saltaire was not to everyone's taste. The art and architectural historian

Sir Nikolaus Pevsner visited the village; in his guide to *The Buildings of England. Yorkshire: The West Riding*, he observed that it was 'monotonous' and that the few decorative features were pedestrian and not indicative of fine taste. Fine or not, the point of the village was to make generations of workers both grateful and industrious. Salt was a businessman and knew that establishing a level of personal control over his workforce would guarantee less trouble from them at work. Should a mill hand be dismissed, his family could also lose their jobs, and their superior homes. Working turnover in Bradford Mills was high outside slump periods, and sacked millworkers could easily take another job, but not so easily find a decent place to live close to work.

> Its fitness for the economical working of a great manufacturing establishment. The estate is bounded by highways and railways which penetrate the very centre of the buildings, and is intersected by both canal and river. Abundance of water is obtained for the use of steam engines, and for the different processes of manufacture.
>
> (Sir William Fairbairn of Manchester on visiting Saltaire, 1850)

Control was evident in the monitoring of workers attending improving activities as well as those which were less 'improving' outside the village. Not only were there no pubs or establishments in which to gossip or gamble; there were also no open meeting spaces in the village. The only places where gatherings could be held were the chapel or park, which were also attended by company employees who noted any inappropriate behaviour. Controls on domestic life, and the provision of access to something extra, apart from keeping the 'best' and 'most respectable' workers, also meant they were less likely to complain or strike.

Saltaire was a case study in site planning and engineering. The buildings are laid out in a structure designed to make the best use of the environment and to manage the workforce. Everything in the village looks towards the mill, its extensive sheds and well-lit rooms, and this was a world away from the factories which had sprung up in central Bradford without much attention to planning or logistics. The size and scale of these works meant they were designed to make use of steam power, supplied from the River Aire. Part of their design involved pumping used water from the scouring and dye works back into the river via lined tunnels. While considered an excellent engineering solution at the time, this inevitably led to the pollution of the waterways, poor sanitary conditions and the spread of diseases such as cholera in the middle of the century.

THE HUDDERSFIELD

At the same time as the Rochdale Canal was started, an even shorter Pennine crossing was proposed – just 20 miles – between Huddersfield and Ashton under Lyne. An original short, private line had already been built in the area by Sir John Ramsden of Longley Old Hall. He was lord of the manor of Huddersfield and, like many West Riding landowners, was ploughing investment and reputation into making 'dirty money'. Many of the local squirearchy families had been involved in commerce for some time, owing to the difficulty in relying on agriculture for profit. The Huddersfield Ramsdens had been profiting from the watermill industry for generations. They had been ennobled after the dissolution of monasteries and were able to buy up land holdings while the Crown desperately needed coin. Sir John's sixteenth-century family motto reads:

Get thy goods truly,
Spend them precisely,
Set they goods dewley,
Lend them thou wisely.

True getting, wise spending,
Have he lytell or moche,

Keepeth a man full ruche,
Until he is ending.

This is the practical Yorkshire mindset: keep your eye on your purse and work hard. The canal Ramsden built took six years to complete and cost him nearly £12,000. He kept detailed records of every expenditure, right down to the ale bought for the workmen and a payment for injury caused to 'Barker, A Labourer, hurt by a fall of earth', for two pounds and two shillings in 1782. The construction of the Huddersfield Canal, however, would cost nearly 20 times as much.

Ramsden had built a short cut of 3.5 miles from the Calder and Hebble waterway to Cooper Bridge, close to Huddersfield, at a time when promoters were trying to get canals in the Lancashire area passed. This was a 'broad cut' designed to take barges up and down between Ramsden's textile suppliers and the 'cloth hall' which he had built in Huddersfield some years earlier. The Ramsden Canal and the extension to the Huddersfield would have a profound impact on the way that the textile trade operated over the next 50 years. The grand hall was designed for manufacturers to set out their wares, but purchasers didn't have to do this once the factory system was properly established. The processing of material under one roof put pressure on the hand-combers and weavers and, once the trade had become fully mechanized, the piece hall would be largely redundant.

In the 1770s, the Ashton Canal Company was pressing for their canal to link to Huddersfield as it represented a short cut to a growing centre and access further on to Hull. A group of shareholders held a meeting in 1793 and asked for a survey for a narrow-gauge (and therefore cost-effective) canal to be carried out by the engineer Benjamin Outram. Knowing the problems that the neighbouring Leeds and Liverpool was having with water supplies at the Pennine summit, Outram suggested that reservoirs could supply the water if a tunnel was dug at Marsden, the highest point on the moor. He planned to use steam engines to make the cutting easier and estimated that a tunnel would take five years to complete. The positive tone of his report was encouraging to investors, pushing the share prices up, and additional funds for a reservoir were raised quickly. This was particularly important for the local mill owners, who were still dependent on waterpower in the hills and needed assurances that courses would not be diverted to supply the canal in dry periods. Standedge (pronounced 'Stannage') Tunnel would become the longest, deepest and highest canal tunnel in Britain – and Outram's plan to build it was so bold it verged on the reckless.

The current line of the canal runs from Ashton under Lyne and Dukinfield in Greater Manchester to Oldham and across Saddleworth Moor to Marsden and Slaithwaite before passing Huddersfield to the River Calder. The tunnel was needed to pass the rocky Saddleworth Moor between Diggle and Marsden. This meant a slow climb of locks to the tunnel, requiring leggers to work beneath the Pennines at a depth of 194 metres. Outram's plans to use pumping engines involved cutting from the western end at Diggle and the Standedge end at the same time, and sinking shafts from the surface to pump out water and loose earth as it was excavated. Digging, however, proved to be expensive and difficult because the method of cut and cover tunnelling could not be used. The route was too deep to be supported and covered by brick arches. The depth alone made it impossible to use the shafts to excavate; they could only be used for pumping out, which was a thankless task as the water gathering on the rainy moors constantly seeped into the excavation. The extra cost of installing and running a fuel-hungry engine for years had not been anticipated, and the work going on at both ends – and under different supervisors – was painfully slow, initially only sinking a yard of shaft per week.

By 1796, Outram's subcontractor on the western end, Thomas Lee, had not completed his part of the work and had run out of money. The canal company itself was in debt to the tune of £30,000. Outram was having considerable trouble with his subcontractors: not only were they running out of money, but there were also complaints about the high rate of accidents caused by black-powder explosives and the number of deaths during the excavation. The investors, too, were protesting about the time being taken to cut the tunnel, and a number of them reneged on their payments. Although the line was in use at either end while the tunnel was being cut, there was dissatisfaction about the loading and unloading required to cut around the tunnel. It soon became clear that not only would the tunnel take much longer than five years to complete but also that its two ends were unlikely to meet cleanly. This was a catastrophe, and Outram resigned his post in 1798, just at the point that the Ashton to Stalybridge section of the neighbouring canal was badly damaged by floodwater.

The line needed another engineer, and quickly. A business-man named John Rooth, who had become involved in the Ashton Canal and operated a carrying business on the Manchester side, wanted to explore the possibilities of taking the carrying trade all the way to Hull via navigations. He and a number of the Ashton Company members met to discuss the problems on the Huddersfield line. Several engineers were hired to replace Outram during the continuation of the works. More important, though, was to get a sensible plan drawn up. An Act of Parliament allowing the raising of further finance was partly dependent on the recommendations of a respected name. Rooth submitted a report on the state of the tunnel and asked for another advisory report from the most famous engineer of the age, Thomas Telford.

Telford, a meticulous Scotsman, had worked across the country and had earned himself a reputation renovating Shrewsbury Castle and several churches, then as a master in building bridges, aqueducts and roads: the bridge he designed to cross the River Severn at Montford was one of 40 he built in Shropshire alone. He also worked on canals, beginning with the Ellesmere, and was asked for his opinion on numerous schemes without being named resident engineer. He was commissioned to prepare a report for Rooth on how to finish Standedge. The report was submitted on 21 January 1807 and predicted a four-year wait for the canal to open. The company had struggled to maintain an engineer of quality on the works, and Rooth stepped in as a de facto supervisor for the final years. He later claimed he was the chief engineer and that, despite Telford's involvement, he had had 'no assistance from an engineer' to complete it. But Telford had made detailed plans and notes and, once the cut had been lined up again, progress was relatively quick, with water supplied from reservoirs on the moors. Still, Standedge, and the Huddersfield Canal, had taken 17 years to complete – more than three times the original estimate by Benjamin Outram.

Standedge Tunnel was finished (see Plate 5) but, 40 years after work had started, the Leeds and Liverpool route still

William Raddon's portrait of Thomas Telford, the most famous engineer of the age. This portrait commemorates his contribution to the Pontcysyllte Aqueduct near Wrexham in north east Wales. Completed in 1805, it was the tallest aqueduct in the world, and still carries 1.5 million litres of water today. Telford lived close by and his house is still visible from the towpath.

wasn't complete. That delay was actually to work in the canal's favour. The original Yorkshire committee proposing the route hadn't been interested in passing through Wigan and on to the Lancashire coalfield. But now, as the canal neared completion, it was obvious that coal had become much more important to serve the rapidly expanding industry. The original route headed north towards Preston, but that was barely started; instead, what had been a spur line towards Wigan and the Lancashire coalfield now became the main route – exactly what the committee of Liverpool investors had been pushing for nearly five decades earlier.

The canal finally joined up at Wigan, and it was one of the most challenging sections of the entire route. At 127 miles, it would be the longest canal in Britain but over its whole length it rose just 487 feet. For the final three-mile stretch at Wigan it rose 200 of those feet, and involved 21 locks.

By 1816, all the difficult geography and climate of the Pennines had been overcome, and they'd been crossed by three canals. The Leeds and Liverpool Canal was the region's main transport artery. Along its route sprang cotton mills, factories, iron mills and warehousing. The volume of goods carried by the canal increased rapidly. Wool, grain and timber were all being transported in bulk, and passengers were being carried as well. Coal remained the most commonly transported cargo. Within a quarter of a century, the Leeds and Liverpool

Canal Company had paid off all its debts, and within 50 years the population of Leeds had trebled. Britain's economy was undergoing an explosive expansion, allowing it to become the first industrial power in the world. Engineers like Thomas Telford had built a network of canals that changed people's lives for ever.

But Telford's legacy does not end with the bridges, aqueducts, roads and canals he built. He was also instrumental in creating a professional body for engineers and encouraging a formal training process. In 1818, the Institute of Civil Engineers was established, bringing an aspect of regulation and security to the profession. It had been the practice for engineers and their assistants to meet informally in pubs before this, and Telford himself regularly attended meetings at the Crown and Anchor tavern on London's Strand, which had been a regular haunt of literary figures such as Coleridge and Samuel Johnson. Telford expressed a desire for an institution of 'more enlarged character' and accepted the post of first President on 21 March 1820.

The new breed of engineers who would study academically as well as 'on the job' were enabled to do so because of lessons learned in the construction of canals. Civil engineering as a profession owed its standing in Victorian and modern society to a handful of pioneers, mostly men of relatively humble birth from the Midlands and rural north. These were the brilliant experimental minds who could find solutions to problems and, by the turn of the nineteenth century, the extraordinary results of their study and work would recast the role of the engineer from that of a 'labouring man' to a modern hero. Men like Brindley, Rennie and Telford became almost godlike in Victorian literature and representation, to the point where their birthplaces as well as their impressive creations became tourist attractions. Victorian audiences were eager to build on the foundations of the men who had built the transport networks and the expectations on a new generation of civil engineers would be put to the test in the age of steam and the development of the railways.

3

THE GEOLOGIST:
THE KENNET AND AVON

SITTING ON THE WEST COAST of England, sheltered from Avonmouth and the sea, the port of Bristol had been wealthy and well populated since medieval times. Strong walls were built to protect the port, its fine castle and its merchants. Such precautions were essential: this was a place which was not only part of one of the country's most important trade routes, but was also a potential defensive point in case of an attack on the island nation. Its wealth as a result of import and export trade had caused landowners and clerics to endow it with eleven churches within the walls and more without, or '*Ultra Avonam*'.

The Mayoral Oath in the 'Mayor's Calendar' written by clerk Robert Ricart in 1478 laid out all the regulations for the citizens, companies and guilds in the town as well as the duties of the new Mayor and boasted that the 'noble and worshipful towwne' enjoyed similar privileges of trade to those of the capital, London. By the time the document was written, however, trade in exports had declined. Luxury imported goods continued to come in, but Bristol had suffered from the development and growth of the port of London and needed to find ways to improve and create new revenue streams.

Development in shipping for deep-sea sailing and the push for exploration in the sixteenth century was the foundation upon which Bristol's fortunes would grow. The late-medieval explorer John Cabot began expeditions from the port at the time the Mayoral Charter was written, as did a number of other adventurers, including a young Christopher Columbus. Further expeditions of trade companies to Africa and the New World would bring back new products such as potatoes and tomatoes as well as exotic spices previously available only via middlemen and foreign traders.

When the sixteenth-century antiquary and scholar John Leland reached Bristol – 'Brightstowe' in his day – he observed that it was 'given much notice as a port of value from the earliest written records'. He described the approach to the town as hard going over 'stony' ground for some three miles, and noted the early linking of the River Frome to the tidal Avon by diverting it manually to allow the building of quays for ships bringing exotic goods, especially from what would soon be known as the New World.

Leland followed the Avon to Bath and Bradford on Avon. He would have been able to go as far as Bath by water had he wished to, and may have been aware of early ideas about creating a link to London by joining the Kennet to the east and the Avon to the west at the Thames after Reading. The merchants of Bristol had long complained of the difficulties in navigating along the Avon from the port because water levels were often not sufficiently high to allow barges to travel and the tidal flow varied to such an extent moving east that it could not be relied on.

Now English merchants could pay for their own ships to travel direct to the source of these goods and thus reduce their costs. As a result, high-ticket items like pepper became much more affordable. In 1400, a pound of pepper might have cost the equivalent of a yearly payment for land tenancy to a manorial lord; by 1700, an artisan worker or shipping clerk in Bristol might be eating a meat pie seasoned with the spice. Fruit, silk and ceramic goods flooded into the country and prompted fashionable copying of exotic eastern designs and Chinese motifs known as chinoiserie. The less palatable side of this explosion of commerce, however, was its reliance on the economic foundation of slavery.

Today, visitors to Bristol can go on the Slave Trade Walk around the city from the centre and the waterside to Clifton's grandiose town houses to discover how and why the triangular trade changed the city in profiting from trade in human beings. The port at Broad Quay was the start and end of the network which took British goods to the West African coast, where they would be traded for enslaved African people, who would then be transported across the Atlantic Ocean to the plantations of North America and the Caribbean. The products grown and harvested by the slaves on the plantations were then shipped to Britain to be sold in bulk to merchants who would warehouse and sell them on domestically. Sugar, rum, tobacco, coffee and chocolate, as well as intensively farmed cotton and other items used in industrial processes such as dyestuffs and hardwoods, were all consumed in great quantity in Georgian England.

A painting of the quayside in around 1785 hanging in the Bristol Museum and Art Gallery (see Plate 7) shows the wooden swing-loading arms along the edge of the water (ready to remove goods) looking up the hill toward St Michael's Church. In the foreground parcels and barrels of luxury products are being inventoried by the employees of merchants who are identified by their brightly coloured silk coats and white periwigs. The servants to the left of the foreground are more simply dressed; one of them is a black teenaged boy, an indication of the presence in the city of people of African origin involved not just in service in grand houses, but in the employ of people whose fortunes were built on the slave trade. Brightly painted shopfronts with awnings stretch all the way up the hill opposite the quay, ready to make the most of trade which was, at the time, second only to London.

The increase in production through the use of generations of slaves in the eighteenth century meant that ships eventually stopped taking the triangular route, instead setting up regular 'shuttle' runs to the colonies, with cargoes loaded to maximum efficiency from the 1750s to 1770s. These journeys could make or break businessmen, who owned, commissioned or held shares in a ship. There was extreme opposition to the anti-slave trade lobby calling for the abolition of the slave trade and for the poor unfortunates within Britain's dominions to be freed. Both sides printed pamphlets, held meetings, campaigned and petitioned Parliament. The Bristolian Merchants and Agents protested that such a measure would affect Britain's trade and continuing development negatively. A leaflet printed for a London meeting of anti-abolitionists rallied its members 'to defeat the injurious tendency of the proposed Abolition of the Trade to Africa for Negro Labourers'. The poem 'Bristolia' by Romaine Joseph Thorne, published in 1794, expresses the conflicting emotions concerning the success of the city and the way its money had been made:

> *Majestic Bristol! To thy happy port,*
> *Prolific COMMERCE makes it's lov'd resort;*
> *Thy gallant ships, with spacious sails, unfurl'd.*
> *Waft, to thy shore, the treasures of the world!*

With each production of the East and West,
Thy favour'd citizen are amply blest;
Thy active sons, unceasingly, are sway'd
By HONOUR, JUSTICE, and a thirst for trade.

When the Act for the Abolition of the Slave Trade was passed in March 1807, it established patrols to stop slaving ships and fined captains found to be carrying human cargo. It would be some years before the ownership of slaves would be outlawed throughout the British dominions, but the effects of restrictions on how businessmen could make their money necessitated the improvement of inland networks in order to get the most from the British consumer market.

Bills to Parliament were put forward to navigate waterways in order to make it easier to get valuable and luxury products further into the country to rival the port of London. There was huge opposition to a number of early bills because landowners who owned turnpike roads and made good revenues from tolls were worried that their trade would be adversely affected.

Other concerns were expressed about the way a navigation for trade might affect the look and feel of the town of Bath, which by the time of the passing of a bill for navigation was becoming renowned as a spa town and the retreat of choice for the cream of London society. To build all the houses, hotels and restaurants needed for a fashionable pleasure palace, Bath would need materials in quantity. An Act to bring materials by watercraft to Bath was passed in 1712, but it would be some years before essential work to open up the river began, with locks being built from Hanham up to the city, charging bargemen tolls for the carriage.

By the mid-1700s both stone and coal were coming into the city and contributing to its growth as well as its wealth, but it was understood that this river could be put to greater use if it could be purchased and artificially cut further east.

Similar arguments were made in the eastern region for using the River Kennet from Reading to link to Newbury. The engineer and surveyor John Hore, a resident of Newbury, realized that the distance would only be 18.5 miles and, although slower and slightly longer than going by road, as a straight path it would be more direct and more secure. This project was not without opposition either and in 1720 the Mayor of Reading headed a mob of locals to do damage to the works where twenty locks up to the town were being constructed. John Hore found himself in hot water over the financial management of the project, while his men were reportedly fighting with bargemen on the opposite side of the navigation who objected to the competition.

One boatman from Maidenhead in Berkshire, along the river navigation bringing his services to the cut, complained to the company that he had received threats of violence:

July 10th 1725

Mr Darvall, wee bargemen of Reading thought to aquaint you before it is too late, Dam you, if you work a bote any more to Newbery we will Kill You if ever you come any more this way, wee was very near to shooting you last time, wee went with pistols loaded and was not too minnits too late. The first time your boat lays at Reading loaded, Dam you, wee will bore holes in her and sink her.

The River Kennet as a single navigation was beset by financial problems. In the mid-1750s a coal merchant named Francis Page was leasing the river and although he had previously tried to buy out the concern, he was refused and decided to go in by the back door by buying up individual shares until, in 1767, he was in control. Under Page, finances were managed better, repairs were made and the navigation leased out again. After Page's death, his sons, Francis and Frederick, took over and were to act on their father's plans to link the two navigations into a single canal called 'the Western'.

Early meetings to plan expansion in 1788 resulted in the partnership of Francis Page II and Charles Dundas (a local MP and Justice of the Peace) and they began to look for other partners and potential shareholders for a 'Western Canal' scheme. Initial surveys were made by a number of engineers to link the rivers in order to encourage subscriptions. To enable the bill, the company needed £75,000; they raised £17,700. This was a huge disappointment considering the amount that would be needed after a bill was actually passed.

Fortune, however, would favour the scheme, as Britain was about to witness an enthusiastic rush of canal building. Canal acts had been passed in England in the 1770s, but the American War of Independence had halted much of the progress. Private enterprise was curtailed as wealthy people with American lands suffered losses, and trade and the political system was disrupted. Potential investors had to secure their holdings during the conflict and were thus less likely to support new schemes in a crisis economy. It would be some years before ambitious projects would start to show how much money could potentially be made. Since the Great Western Canal (as it was first called) was one of the earliest begun, those would-be investors had very little precedent for the construction or maintenance of such works within budget. The Bridgewater Canal in Manchester had proved a success, though, and the subsequent rewards persuaded most potential investors. Canal building began in a frenzy. In 1793 alone, 20 canals were authorized by Parliament. Even though things calmed down quite quickly in the following two years, it was easy to see how people could get carried away. It was a classic example of a speculative bubble, and it left some of those caught up in the craze high and dry.

Before the Western Canal scheme had actually begun to look for investors, the men of Bristol were subscribing to a project to link Bristol to the Severn. Although it was never built, every subsequent proprietors' meeting was crowded with potential investors trying to buy shares. Their hope was to mount a hostile takeover of the fledgling scheme for the Western Canal. A group of interested men advertised a meeting to divulge plans and gather signatures for a canal from Bristol into Wiltshire, to be held in the town of Devizes in order to throw people off the scent of the real scheme. The businessmen had in fact already gathered in Bristol at a pub called the White Lion, where they had planned to raise the necessary fees and bid for the buyout. The effect of the ruse was to fill Devizes with hopeful speculators all competing for food, lodging and transport. A shambolic meeting was arranged to pacify the restless crowd, but no plans were laid out. Those who attended returned home empty-handed and out of pocket.

The event was much satirized in the press, with a poem later appearing in one newspaper called 'Mad Gallop, or The Trip to Devizes' by Romaine Joseph Thorne in 1794:

> *Where those who in canal, a share,*
> *Would fain secure, must fast repair*
> *Or sure Miss Jenny is the toast,*
> *The shares would quick be all engrossed;*

For someone had the hint giv'n out
At once is emptied, every stable,
of bone and mare, to journey able,
And even such as, groaning lie,
In stagger, dire, their strength must try.

(Bristol Central Library Collections)

The Avon was sold eventually, and an offer of sale of the Kennet made by the Page brothers. Shortly afterwards, in September 1793, the committee met to make some changes to the original proposal, to reroute it and rename it the Kennet and Avon Canal Company. The company would receive assent to begin their work in 1794, with the first sod being cut in October. At the same time, a number of other canal projects were being worked on in the immediate vicinity. One of these, the Somerset Coal Canal, would prove interesting to the project as well as to a generation of engineers to come.

THE ENGINEER

The senior engineer on the Kennet and Avon project was appointed in May. John Rennie was born in East Lothian, a rural and relatively impoverished part of the Scottish borders, at Phantassie near Harrington. The youngest son of a farmer who had died when the boy was only five, Rennie was able to go to the local Kirk school where he was taught enough to go on, after some initial training in the 'mechanical arts', to school in Dunbar. An inspector of the Dunbar fisheries had occasion to visit the 'Burgh Schools' in the town and remarked in a document published in 1779 that he had noticed a boy of 17 who was especially gifted. 'One would have imagined him a second Newton,' he remarked.

> No problem was too hard for him to demonstrate. With a clear head, a decent address, and a distinct delivery, he gave ready solutions to questions in natural and experimental philosophy, and also the reasons of the connection between causes and effects, the power of gravitation, &c., in so masterly and convincing a manner, that every person present admired such an uncommon stock of knowledge amassed at his time of life. If this young man is spared, and continues to prosecute his studies, he will do great honour to his country.
>
> (Samuel Smiles, *Lives of the Engineers*)

Rennie had a remarkable mind, enough so for his school-master, on being offered a promotion elsewhere, to suggest the teenager as his replacement as mathematics teacher. Life as

John Rennie was one of the most famous names associated with British canals.
He was celebrated for his prolific works reflecting personal design and the desire
to create something that would be admired in the years to come. He is best
known for his work on bridges, specifically Waterloo and New London Bridge.

a schoolmaster was not to be, though: Rennie instead returned to the workshop of Andrew Meikle, a millwright.

Meikle was an inventor and 'machine man' in his own right, credited with developing useful mechanical solutions in agriculture, including a 'thrashing machine'. Although the millwright was never to make his fortune by inventing things, he did help to develop innovative ways of building waterwheels and watercourses to run water-powered factories in the area, and Rennie learned first-hand about the nature of waterways and how they could be 'cut' and manipulated in order to get the best use from them. Part of this came from acquiring an understanding of the land and the hands-on approach employed in adapting and building as well as designing machinery. This experience on the job allowed him to earn enough money to support himself at Edinburgh College under the tutelage of two renowned thinkers by the name of Dr Robison and Dr Black, who were students of 'natural philosophy' and chemistry.

At the time, mechanical engineering could not be studied at university. Those sciences that aided in the study of medicine, for which Edinburgh was the principal place of learning, were more acceptable, and scientific writing was a field that was growing in influence, with professional bodies espousing the study of the physical world and the application of mathematics and theory to everyday life and problems. But all that was a far cry from teaching a student the mechanical arts and the practice of engineering.

After study, and further practice in mechanical design, Rennie set out on a journey that was to change the course of his life. In 1783, he began visiting sites of particular interest in terms of invention. In Lancashire he studied the work of James Brindley in building the Bridgewater Canal, and visited other newly industrialized towns to view their factories and bridges and the new condensing steam engines being built at the Boulton and Watt workshops in Soho, Birmingham.

Making new connections and learning from them, Rennie quickly started to receive job offers; at the age of just 23 he was commissioned by the Town Council of Edinburgh to build a bridge and docks at Leith off the turnpike road. He would later put his success down to a commission he received, after working with Boulton and Watt, to build a plant called Albion Mills close to Paddington in London. This established his reputation as a reliable and knowledgeable engineer. In an age when there were no 'professional' engineers, just men who could 'do', men such as Rennie were in short supply.

Rennie was appointed surveyor on the Kennet and Avon Canal project in 1794, as was William Jessop. Jessop was a veteran of the West and East India Docks, and the Grand Junction, both in London, and had worked on remodelling Bristol Harbour. He and Rennie now produced plans for the canal and advice on the width of the cut as well as how to deviate to avoid problematic areas where tunnels might have to be dug. Rennie planned to go ahead with building a canal wide enough to take heavy barges; this would be more expensive to construct than a narrow-gauge cut, but, by taking boats with up to 50 tons of goods (double the amount on a narrow canal), it would ultimately be more profitable.

He also realized that altering the original route of the Western would make it quicker to cut, as well as avoid some of the obvious problems with lack of tidal flow and provision of water. He planned to divert at Crofton, building locks and an engine house to pump water and ensure good supply, instead of digging a tunnel, like the one at Harecastle on the Trent and Mersey; this would have been more expensive and would have taken far too long to construct. Work on the digging was to start, as with other projects, at 'both ends' at once – from Bradford on Avon and Newbury – to meet in the middle and make the best use of completed parts of the line. Each end of the cut would join the rivers and be developed into a single waterway. This plan meant two teams working at far remove both from each other and the watchful eyes of the committee.

This might have been easier to manage if the distance had been shorter or Rennie able to take full control, but by now he was being called away regularly to advise other companies on their building projects. Apart from his work on canals, surveying the Rochdale and Lancaster Canal and building impressive aqueducts over the rivers Wyre and Lune, he was by now an experienced builder of grand ornamental bridges, including new ones at Southwark and Waterloo in London.

One of the biggest difficulties on the Kennet and Avon work would be the anchoring of the wide-spanning Dundas aqueduct with iron rods into the body and pillars of the structure. There were many problems with getting the canal to remain watertight and dealing with slippage as a result of leaks through puddled clay linings. As Rennie tended to delegate to other engineers working on specific sections, he was not always present and didn't oversee much of the day-to-day work. He needed a 'resident' to oversee operations and put his plans into action. But just as Rennie's work was in demand, so was that of the other engineers who might otherwise have remained working on a line until its completion.

Smaller firms tendered for the right to work a 'section' and, although the physical work proceeded, the crews were soon to run into difficulties. Rennie hired local companies and some of them, eager to take full advantage of the years of work the canal offered, tendered for more sections than they were able to complete. Being in a rural location, it was not always possible to attract enough labour either. In addition there were frequent failures to make full surveys before starting a new section. As the Kennet and Avon was an early undertaking, there was a great deal of delay and expense thanks to a lack of experience and knowledge of the terrain through which the route was being cut. The area was already known for its stone quarries, and this should have indicated that full surveys as well as bores were needed to check for hidden levels of bedrock. Instead, such discoveries were made while cutting was in progress, and the necessity of blasting through was time-consuming, expensive and dangerous.

The stages of the new canal proceeded slowly and became increasingly expensive. Labour was short and cutting slow, not helped by the payment of the men in promissory notes when money was tight. Apart from encountering hidden bedrock where it was thought cutting might be easy, an absence of the clay Rennie had hoped to find meant that the bricks he had planned to manufacture for linings and building would not be available locally. Making bricks would have been costly in itself, but bringing them across country was even more so. Additional problems were caused by the nature of the Wiltshire soil: it was chalky and difficult to make watertight, even with the use of clay linings. Water gathering under cut limestone seeped into the earth, creating conditions for collapse and a greater need to shore up.

To make matters worse, there were discrepancies in the treasurer's accounts. For a while it seemed that Francis Page would have to sell the river to pay the debt; in the end, it was agreed that the Page brothers would instead relinquish a large number of shares. Some financial errors – and the Pages' inability to explain them – might have stemmed from the fact that, as construction was under way, a number of landowners were charging high prices for the canal to cross their estates. Not only that, some of them objected to being within sight of the workings and, if they didn't oppose and deny it outright, some placed conditions on permission to cut. One of the conditions of an Act of Improvement made in 1796, for example, was a demand that the new engine pump house at Crofton should be made to consume the smoke it generated, rather than sending it in a vertical plume that might spoil the view of the Earl of Ailesbury. Interestingly, although in 1793–4 there had been vocal opposition from landowners and businessmen making toll road profits, within a year the *Bristol Journal* was reporting that the difficulties had been overcome and that landowners were actively promoting the benefits of the line. And the need for a 29-strong flight of locks along the route between Devizes and Rowde in Wiltshire (the Caen Hill Locks) meant that there was now mounting pressure to get as much of the canal open as possible east and west.

TROUBLE STARTS

The Kennet and Avon Canal was now so over budget that Rennie had to tell the committee in 1800, and again in 1804, that more investment – hundreds of thousands of pounds' worth – would be needed, which meant floating more shares on the market. At least £140,000 had been spent on unforeseen costs such as repairs, replacements and on inflated prices for crossing private land. In 1798 Dudley Clark, Rennie's man on the ground, was dismissed for overspending.

With hindsight and the benefit of fast and reliable testing methods, it is clear that some of the materials used were unsuitable. Rennie had planned linings and buildings in bricks, but he was encouraged by the canal committee to design for the use of locally quarried stone. The local stone was limestone, which immediately caused problems: under pressure, water forces its way into pockets within the unseasoned stone, pushing air out and gradually rendering the stone unfit for use. All the stonework on the scheme needed regular repairing and sometimes replacement, as it was liable to blow.

Building locks to raise craft to the Caen summit would be difficult and the 29 locks required would have to be placed close together. Brick would be needed for this because of the regularity of use and changes in water level. Bricks had to be made on site to make this viable, and sufficient quantities of clay were at last found to make this possible. Where Rennie was forced to build with stone, he had to make the best use of the local resource, which was not ideal for the task and had to be seasoned before it was submerged in order to work well.

There wasn't time to prepare the locally quarried stone for installation, which meant that there were significant leaks and numerous occasions when masonry was damaged as a result of the poor quality of the materials. It had been hoped that, as well as supplying the works and contributing to the local economy, an outlet might be established to sell stone quarried nearby from the canal itself. Even stone for masonry and linings had to be brought via the Avon from the Hanham quarry in Bristol, adding further to the cost.

Eventually, in 1801, the committee had to open its own quarry, which provided much better quality stone. The quarry was connected to the diggings by what was by then a fairly common way of moving goods to water: a wooden 'tram' track leading to the loading wharfs at Murhill. Rennie's continuing efforts to persuade the canal committee to change their minds about stone were still being ignored. The ideas of other engineers Rennie had worked with were also summarily dismissed by his bosses.

In the later years of canal building stone quality was improved, but it was still found to leak, and silting and watertightness were also problems that were expensive to put right. Rennie was also worried about the degree of regular maintenance required to keep the canal safe, as there were serious safety implications along the route. The Caen Hill lock flight (see Plate 8) is one of the most picturesque parts of the man-made construction on the entire route and was also one of the most important parts of the journey to get right. Rennie argued that the works already completed on the aqueducts had shown the 'badness of the stone' in frost damage during the winters as well as the buckling from water pressure. This had been especially true on the Dundas aqueduct near Avoncliffe. Somewhat wearily, Rennie wrote again to the committee in March 1803:

> I feel it my duty to repeat again to the committee, what I have frequently done before, the propriety of again considering whether or not it would be better to use Bricks generally instead of stone in the Works which are yet to do.

The compromise of using Bath stone quarried from Hanham for the Dundas or Avoncliffe Aqueduct would not work for the locks at Devizes; they would require clay in order to function properly. This was the last section to be completed and the reportedly chance find, while digging it out, of suitable puddling clay was to prove useful as the middle section required much more lining work due to the nature of the chalk hills. This resulted in the Devizes Brick and Tile Works being built close to the site, operated by R. B. Mullings, in 1809. Two million bricks made on site were used to line the two-barge Bruce Tunnel (also called the Savernake Tunnel) below Wolf Hall and the Crofton pumping station, on the lands of Thomas Bruce, Earl of Ailesbury. The only tunnel on the canal, its inscription on completion in 1810 read:

> In testimony of the uniform and effectual support of Thomas Bruce, Earl of Ailesbury and Charles Lord Bruce, his son, through the whole progress of this great and national work by which a direct communication of Water was opened between the cities of London and Bristol, Anno Domini MDCCCX

That the project had received 'uniform support' could hardly be said to be true; the Earl had been on the committee for the early Western Canal and obviously saw the potential of the construction, but he didn't want to see evidence of it every day. A tunnel was not required across the land, as the going was fairly flat. Trees would have to have been felled, but the Earl's requirements meant that extra work and expense was incurred at a time when the canal was already well over budget. By now, it was clear that an additional £200,000 would be needed and the company still had debts at the time.

The total cost of the project was £979,314.00 7s 4d. That's over £68,000,000 in today's money, although such a conversion only takes into account the relative sum and not the cost of goods and services compared to those available in the 1790s. Labour was cheap and there were no restrictions on hours worked or methods used, much less insurance or health and safety as on a modern construction project.

The canal was finally ready, with its pumping house for water supply, its impressive flight of locks and grand and imposing aqueducts, in December 1810. So much had been spent and there was such a level of anxiety about profitability that the shareholders and members held their breaths and did not organize any form of grand opening or announcements, waiting to see if the expense had truly been worth it.

THE SOMERSET COAL CANAL

Around this same period, in 1805, the Somerset Coal Canal opened on the joint of the site of Rennie's famous Dundas Aqueduct, named after the chairman of the Kennet and Avon, Charles Dundas. Rennie had surveyed both canals initially in the same period, and they were made to meet at a junction in order to expand the movement of the coal and compete with Welsh companies.

It had been acknowledged for some time that 'a successful canal must have coal at the heels of it'. Coal proved to be the top carriage for most canals, necessary for the manufacture of anything and everything in the factories as well as in heating and cooking for the wider population. Coal production doubled in the 50 years up to 1800 as a result of mass mechanization and changes in the cities, and it continued to grow at stages leading up to the establishment of the railways.

The sixteenth century saw the growth of coal as a fuel, and the production of coke for the smelting of different types of iron ore. Expansion through growth of cities, commercial markets and developments in shipping and roadbuilding led to innovations in machinery and in processes which all relied on the availability of coal rather than wood and charcoal.

In the sixteenth and seventeenth centuries, most coal mining was carried out using the bell pit or 'patch' recovery method in drifts at the edge of a coal seam. The technology had not been developed to mine at great depth, and the thousands of bell pits all over local mineral-rich areas were worked by small teams. At only 20 to 30 feet, they were not deep and were quickly worked out as the sides of the pits were propped up by pillars of coal already excavated or by wooden stakes. Gradually new methods of post and shaft and long-wall mining were developed, to allow for deeper digging and for air to flow through the workings by use of intake and outtake draughts, operated by gates.

The Somerset Coal Canal was dug in regions where the main profit came from coal, and this was long before areas such as the West Midlands, South Wales, South Yorkshire and the North East of England became major coal producers. Every area needed to exploit coal if it could be found locally. Somerset had a number of mines but could not compete with the coalfields further north, especially by the time of the expansion of the railways, but in the mid-1700s it had established a regional trade and was keen to make the best of it.

As they expanded and were sunk to greater depths, for most mines ways had to be found to address the issues of drainage as well as ventilation and the moving of coal. Excavating and digging tunnels meant that miners had to remove groundwater and pump out any found at deep levels as well as any which might flood workings in regions already prone to waterlogging. Early shallow mines could avoid being flooded by the digging of ditches, but deeper pits required a solution that worked underground.

The coal mine owners and shareholders also needed to find a way to get their product to Bath. By the 1790s, Bath had become wealthy and plenty of coal was needed to heat both the accommodation for visitors and facilities at the mineral spa pools in which they came to bathe. The history of Bath contains one of the earliest references to the use of coal in the Roman occupation of the town they named *Aqua Sulis*; it was mined to heat the temple around which the modern city's tourist industry is based. The Somersetshire Coal Canal came together with the Kennet and Avon at the west end of the aqueduct by the basin close to Limpley Stoke. The coal mines were something on which the Kennet and Avon committee hoped to capitalize, and they raised no objections to an independent line, considering they might have shared regular business.

Only one of two planned lines was constructed, because of steep inclines at a point called Combe Hay. There was not sufficient water to raise boats and an early boat lift was put in place, in the form of a floating caisson. The mechanism worked by navigating a boat into a cistern and a watertight box, then lowering the caisson on a rack and pinion system until it lined up with a short tunnel and the correct level of water. It wasn't particularly successful: it was laborious, expensive and dangerous to operate. The chamber of the 'hydrostatic lock' was not able to cope with the pressure of water as well as craft, and there had been considerable delay in construction anyway. The caisson was later demolished and replaced with an inclined plane on to which coal could be loaded and unloaded. This was also time-consuming and expensive and eventually the proprietors had to admit to failure; they would have to return to the tried and tested means of the lock system.

All the problems encountered in cutting canals in this part of the country had taught the fledgling engineers some important lessons. If such problems were to be avoided on other projects, extensive surveys would need to be undertaken, and –

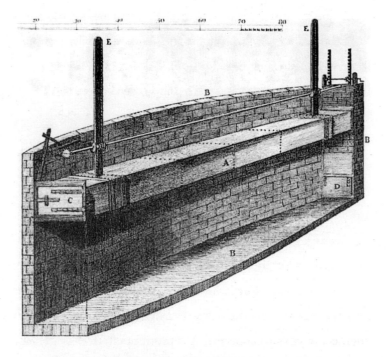

The caisson lock designed by Robert Weldon – a watertight box to contain a boat, in a cistern of water over 27 metres (80 feet) deep. It allowed a boat to be floated in through a sliding door, and lowered using a rack and pinion system to slide out of the opposite door, in order to cope with the steep gradient at Combe Hay.

rather than simple bores made prior to digging – plans would have to be drawn up based on a scientific understanding and appreciation of the geology and ecology of the environment.

> The strata between Wootton Rivers and Devizes being mostly open chalk and sand, great difficulty was experienced in forming a water-tight bed for the canal, as well as in preventing slips of the adjacent ground. At that part of the line which lies between the river Biss and Trowbridge, the works were carried along the face of a steep slippery hill. Then near Bradford the cutting is mostly through open rock, and beyond that through beds of tough clay interspersed with strata of fuller's earth.
>
> (Samuel Smiles, *Lives of the Engineers*)

The word 'strata' was coined by William Smith, an Oxfordshire man who had worked on the Somerset Coal Canal. As with other projects in which he became involved, John Rennie had not stayed with the Somerset; instead he hired Smith as engineer to carry out surveys. A young student of mathematics and geometry, Smith had been cared for by an uncle from an early age after the death of his father. At the age of 18, in 1787, he was taken on as an assistant for works to map and enclose land for one Edward Webb in Stow-on-the-Wold in

Gloucestershire. From this point Smith began to keep diaries noting interesting natural phenomena and the regularity with which they occurred. Primarily, clients were interested in the improvement of land, with particular regard to the methods of 'scientific' farming on a grander scale. Surveys enabled landowners to find ways of draining marshland for planting and grazing, as well as increasing yield for the tables of the growing population.

> To the members of the Norfolk Agricultural Society
>
> Gentlemen, REGARDING you as the legitimate Patrons of all works, which tend to the laudable purpose for which your society has been instituted, I most anxiously solicit the favour of dedicating these sheets to you, convinced that I cannot obtain a more honoreable sanction.
>
> … Of this honour I shall ever be most proud, and I will endeavor to deserve it, by exerting whatever talent I may posess, in the way most conducive to your generous wishes – to improve the condition of mankind, by increasing the produce of the land.

It was Webb who first sent Smith to work in Somerset to survey the estate of an aristocratic family. Living in the area, Smith encountered the mining works. Studies of pits and orders of clays and coal deposits formed the basis for models he made and used in subsequent years. John Rennie met Smith during this period and engaged him as an assistant, first on the Coal Canal, and later the Kennet and Avon, where he surveyed private lands to resolve issues of drainage and bring about improvement; he had also worked locally, in some cases preventing the foundations of buildings being lost in land slips. After the disasters on the neighbouring canal, and as an employee of the coal mines in the area, Smith realized that

William 'Strata' Smith, who came to be called
the 'Father of English Geology'.

there was something special about the formations of rock and soil as well as types of clay and minerals underground. His employers therefore sent him to other parts of the country, specifically to observe and study other canal projects.

Smith travelled to Coalbrookdale in the Midlands in 1791 and observed the tunnels on the Shropshire Canal, as well as mechanical machinery used at the local coal mines. He had already noticed that coal behaved in patterns: where particular conditions were found it became easier to predict the grades and extent of a coal or an iron seam. On his travels and afterwards, Smith wrote down his observations and concluded that the regularity of conditions for particular layers of materials could not be ignored. He made drawings, and interviewed experienced miners about their knowledge of seams and excavation, such as how deep a seam might go, or how minerals were best extracted in safety. When he surveyed the canal, the rocks he encountered yielded fossils, types of which were found at different levels, proving that there must be something uniform about the type of rock they were in, the age of the rock and how it would appear at the same depths in the landscape. He also made detailed observations of what happened to water depending on the soil and mineral content.

Although he became increasingly interested in studying the fossils found in the ground, Smith's initial motivation was to use the evidence gathered in full and precise surveying and the compiling of maps, measurements and charts to determine if an area was likely to contain mineral beds. Later he would become known as 'Strata' Smith and the 'Father of English Geology', although canal histories seldom mention him other than to note that he was dismissed from the Somerset due to 'financial irregularity'. It would appear that, given charge of purchase funds for land on which to expand, he spent some of them on a home for himself and was unable to account for the shortfall to the committee. After his dismissal, Smith was, like Rennie, able to find other employers who valued his skills, but it would be some years before the magnitude of his findings would become clear.

A child's guide to coal and coal mining published in the 1940s, called *A Ramble Among Our Industries*, sets out to explain the basics of coal mining. It suggests an experiment:

> Take a little coarse sand and drop it into a tumbler about three parts full of water. After an hour or so, when the sand has quite settled, remove the water by means of a siphon. In a second tumbler, mix finer sand with water and pour this into the first. Let the second layer settle on the first one and again, draw off the water. Repeat this with finer sand still. In this way you will note how the different layers of

sand form, and see how like they are to rocky strata. Geologists have found that all rocks that lie in strata have been formed in the Earth's crust by the action of water.

In certain areas, such as along the coasts looking at levels in open cliffs, Smith was able to see such formations, but on a plain they were more difficult to discern. In looking for coal, which was formed by the degrading of vegetation trapped under beds of sand and mud as well as layers of swamp or marshy water, surveyors began to understand how coal was formed, and the ways to find different types of coal, by studying the earth around a particular source. The quality of coal varied and different types were used for different aspects of manufacturing depending on their hardness, how deeply buried they were and in what chemical conditions they were found. Such conditions, which were now predictable, meant that mining for minerals with specific properties – such as engine coal which would burn solidly to produce power at high temperatures – was possible. Different areas and their geological background would therefore be expected to offer up different results as well as present different problems. Smith had observed that by taking measurements, noting peaks and troughs in the land and comparing these to his findings in the earth, he could determine the way the land mass had shifted, and caused some of the physical characteristics of the regions in which he travelled. He climbed to the top of York Minster to get a view from the highest vantage point of the angles of rock formation towards the south. There, he observed the formation of the rocky countryside of the dales and realized that the change from north to south confirmed what he had suspected from previous tests: that the southern part of the country must have split away from the rest of Europe in ancient times, as its rock formations had fewer strata, or levels of deposit, and so had to be more recent than those in the north.

William Smith's legacy goes beyond his breakthrough in understanding the geological 'history' of the country, or his advice on how to find a way through the earth to exploit it. His work and access to his collections of fossils prompted others to study geology and physical sciences permanently. He had taken one step closer to the professionalization of the subject and the wider world's understanding of it. In the eighteenth century there were no professional or 'qualified' men in such fields, but that didn't mean that ideas were not disseminated or that all men who worked on major engineering projects and in surveying were unschooled or from working-class backgrounds. Schools and universities did not teach subjects which were considered 'manual crafts', preferring to concentrate on the classical subjects of theology, philosophy and literature. This started to change following the work of Smith and others like him. Theories could be tested and, gradually, centres of learning began to understand the need to prove a hypothesis in the sphere of working and everyday lives.

People who were interested in scientific subjects and the answers to puzzling questions tended to seek out clever men from whom to gather evidence. Scientific salons or societies sought to understand the world better by working together with industrialists and their employees, and mechanics institutes opened to spread such ideas beyond the privileged university educated to the workers and labourers who, like Rennie and Smith, were learning on the job.

In 1815, after his work on the Somerset and other canals, Smith produced his masterpiece, a national geological map of stratification called (in abbreviated form) 'A delineation of the strata of England and Wales with part of Scotland', for the Geological Society (see Plate 9). Although overlooked at the time, Smith's geological insights would prove enormously influential to people like Charles Darwin, who applied similar principles to the plants and animals of the world, tracing their evolution over huge spans of time. Darwin's grandfather, Erasmus, a contemporary of William Smith's, was an inquiring mind who participated in the 'scientific and philosophical' debates and symposia in the Midlands. Working as a specialist surveyor on contract allowed Smith to produce his map. The findings of his surveys were also to go on to inform the drafting of valuable land maps and later on methods of understanding and plotting archaeological discoveries.

On his travels, collecting samples and fossils, Smith made good use of his orphaned nephew John Phillips and niece Anne, to whom he entrusted his collection for cataloguing. John himself became a geologist and lectured at the University of Oxford, despite not having a degree himself. He became well respected and wrote extensively on the subject, as well as publishing a memoir of his uncle after William's death in 1839.

Smith's diaries and papers, including maps made, survive today at the Oxford University Museum, donated by his nephew, who wrote of having destroyed some of his letters detailing aspects of his uncle's personal life and financial situation. Intriguingly, he referred to William's life as having been seen by others as problematic, but that William himself had only 'regretted' that aspects of it had prevented him from doing all he wanted in life. He may have been referring to his relationship with his wife, Rebecca, who apparently suffered from mental health problems, and his ability to make and manage money successfully. John Phillips was concerned that his uncle was unable to make the best use of his position and work and that his publications and maps cost him too much to produce for too little return. Smith's work took him all over the country and the cost of maintaining his lifestyle meant that often he couldn't pay debts and spent time in the debtors' prison.

Smith never made much money from his work or private writings. The famous 1815 map 'A delineation of the strata of England and Wales with part of Scotland' was to cost him more than he made from the Geological Society, an organization he was never invited to join. Recognition came late in the award of the Wollaston Medal by the Society in 1831; in a sense they were forced to do so because of the growing popularity and refining of Smith's work during the period of expanded research into the subject at the dawn of the Victorian age. But by then Smith's financial difficulties had forced him to sell the majority of his fossil and specimen collection to the Treasury, which purchased it for the British Museum. A condition of the sale was the cataloguing of the items purchased and the deposit of notes and explanations of the research, which prompted Smith to write a number of papers in later life relating to them.

> The novel and interesting description of near seven hundred species of fossil shells, zoophites and other organized fossils, found in England and Wales, and collected in identification of the Strata, refers particularly to the specimens of geological collection deposited in the British Museum ...
>
> The copious reference to the Stratum which contain the fossils, and to the individual specimens

of the collection, which is intended to be publically
exhibited in the British Museum, seemed to render
figures of them unnecessary.

(William Smith's Introduction to *Stratigraphical System of
Organized Fossils*, 1817)

Smith continued to work, but old age made it more difficult
for him to tour the country giving lectures to the growing
numbers of students and enthusiasts who could put his
discoveries to use.

The Scarborough Rotunda Museum houses some of the
fossils the family collected and worked with. Not only were
students of mathematics and science to learn much from
them, but the expanded knowledge of what they were and how
they could be used to understand the earth contributed vastly
to the passion for private and public collecting. Universities,
societies and wealthy benefactors paid for scholars to travel
to Europe and beyond to compare samples and specimens
of plant, marine and animal life. For some years it had
been fashionable for private enthusiasts and 'gentlemen of
quality' not only to support such endeavours, but to collect
pieces themselves in 'cabinets of curiosity' to show to friends
and colleagues. The ownership and displaying of items of
antiquity or rare fossils reflected both taste and intellect and,
thanks to men like Smith and those who developed his work

further over the next century, collectors were better able to understand the nature of the objects they owned. Many such private collections would go on to form the basis of specialist collections in public museums in the later nineteenth and twentieth centuries as museums and galleries began to expand and spread outside London and the university towns.

The observation of how the land looked and how it worked in the Industrial Revolution would allow further exploration into the way minerals could be mined. The excavation of deep coal beds in the mid-nineteenth century, the digging of large reservoirs to provide clean drinking water for towns and the building of rail networks were all directly influenced by the scientific approach embodied in the work of William Smith.

4

THE WORKERS: THE MANCHESTER SHIP CANAL

I'm a navvy, I work on the Ship Canal
I'm a tipper and live in a hut with my Sal

('The Manchester Ship Canal Navvy' by 'The Ship Canal Navvy Poet')

By THE LATE 1800s Britain's extensive network of canals was almost complete. Man-made waterways criss-crossed the country for nearly 5000 miles. But the gangs of navvies who'd changed the landscape of the country would have one last triumph as the century came to a close. One final, giant project that would be hailed as the greatest engineering feat of the Victorian age – the Manchester Ship Canal.

Travellers' guides to the waterways, or even histories of the canals in England, make relatively little reference to the Manchester Ship Canal. Indeed, some enthusiasts don't consider this one of the 'proper' canals at all, because it was designed for ocean-going vessels rather than narrow boats. Running parallel to and crossing over the other earlier undertakings of the Sankey (or St Helens) Canal and the famous Bridgewater Canal, the MSC is nevertheless regarded as a separate waterway in its own right.

The cutting (if not the idea) for this development didn't commence until well after the canal-building boom was over.

Even compared to canal developments of the later nineteenth and early twentieth centuries, the MSC stands alone, in that it was not an amalgamation or a conversion of an existing waterway, but a purpose-built solution keeping Manchester's finances 'afloat'.

What, though, had put Manchester in the position of being a large industrial hub in the North West? And how did this great late Victorian engineering project ever get off the ground?

Manchester Piccadilly in the 1890s – before bombings in the Second World War impacted upon the way the centre looked. At boom production in the last half of the eighteenth century, there was an increased interest in the prospect of a new waterway.

THE MAKING OF MANCHESTER

Looking at maps of the fifteenth and sixteenth centuries you could be forgiven for thinking that Manchester was a place of no particular significance. The 1630 regional hundreds map of the County Palatine of Lancaster marks out Rochdale, Blackburn and Salford as large landholdings and more significant centres than poor Manchester, close to the border with the County of Cheshire.

From 1535 to 1543, the antiquary and scholar John Leland recorded the counties of England and Wales he passed through in order to make a survey of the kingdom for Henry VIII. The Tudor monarchs were not just keen to establish a better understanding of the kingdom and the potential revenue streams to the crown after years of impoverishing civil war; they also wanted to make their mark. The 1630 map lays out the terms of the 'joinying of the red and white rose in one', to establish the Tudor claim to the throne through Henry VII's marriage to Elizabeth of York in 1486.

Anxious to map out the towns and districts of an expanding kingdom and concerned with the promotion of trade, Leland arrived in Lancashire. There he noted:

> Manchestre on the South side of Irwel River
> stondith in Salfordshire, and is the fairest, best

buildid, quikest, and most populous tounne in al Lancashire; yet is in hit but one paroche chirch.

Ther be divers stone bridges in the tounne, but the best is of iii [three] arches is over Irwel, cawlid Salford Bridge. This bridge dividith Manchestre from Salford, the wich is as a large suburbe to Manchestre.

Leland's impression that Salford was just a 'suburb of Manchester', rather than existing in its own right, would not be popular with its citizens (then or now), but his description disproves the notion that Manchester only became worthy of note after the industrial boom of the eighteenth century.

When Leland described a place favourably, it was nearly always in terms of its being 'quik', which had less to do with size than with appetite for hard work and business. In Tudor times Manchester had already become a town with great opportunity for growth. This was in no small part to do with the three main rivers serving the area. The entire region of Lancashire was considered remote in the early sixteenth century, and the roadways which existed were notoriously difficult to negotiate, especially over high rocky ground.

Waterways were not much better in the earlier days either. They were sustaining for communities and for localized industrial process, but were not yet capable of being used effectively as 'navigations'. Leland also noted that the River Irwell was not navigable for larger craft and was impeded by rocks, since Manchester 'Stondith on a hard rokke of stone, els Irwel, as wel apperith in the west ripe, had beene noiful to the tounne'. He informed readers that, at such places, fords could easily be made over the rivers, hence local names like Salford.

It was especially difficult, though, to make the northern rivers navigable for barges due to their sources high in the Pennine hills. Here the water runs quickly at points until it hits a plateau and evens out. What's more, the setting up of weirs on higher ground to run waterwheels for mills meant that, as water was being diverted, it might not keep levels high enough along the course. As the sea level fell considerably over two centuries, it became steadily more difficult to move goods along the river systems due to lack of reliable water level.

In this environment, engineering the lie of the waterway was essential to avoid vessels bound for the coast being stranded by lack of water. The use of an ancient method of lock systems called a 'pound lock' allowed the water to be levelled off through steep inclines, while conserving it to be reused and still keeping flow steady. These locks were deep enough for merchants' ships to pass. Successful experiments with these measures meant that Manchester's rivers could be engineered more effectively and so its specialist products could reach their markets.

In the 1600s cotton began to be developed in the region, having been first introduced to Britain by Levantine merchants, selling to London markets. Lancashire's physical landscape of steep inclines and fast-flowing water sources – as well as the climate, which was cooler and damper than elsewhere in the United Kingdom – suited the processing and piecing of cottons in manufacture. In the south of the region, where Lancashire met Cheshire and Merseyside, other textiles were being produced. The low-lying and often marshy ground in this area was better for the growing of natural-fibre plants such as flax, from which linen was produced. Used in underwear and shirts, linen was light in weight, comfortable and easy to wash. It wasn't very warm, however, and that necessitated the wearing of layers of homespun and woven woollens of varying quality.

Expertise in working with both natural wool and plant fibres developed even further with seventeenth-century experiments in cotton manufacture. Cotton was on the market even in the 1300s, mostly purchased and traded from London, after its arrival from the Middle East. It was also used for underclothes and shirts, but could only be afforded by the wealthiest in the land. Gradually, though, commercial links opened up, and, as British companies were granted overseas business licences, so the trade in cotton expanded. The growing and development of eastern cotton plants and the cultivation of cotton on a

1. Paddington Basin, 1801. The location of the Grand Junction here allowed easy movement of goods onto central London's roads, for distribution and later to the rail network.

2. Paddington Basin, 1840. Just forty years after the Grand Junction opened, and despite the leisure use of canals being limited until the later twentieth century, early 'packet' or day trip boats ran from points of interest. Victorian Londoners made good leisure use of the waterways in summer, often to the annoyance of those working on them.

3. The Braunston bridges from Hassell's *Tour of the Grand Junction*, published in 1819. Hassell was surprised at the scenery to be viewed by boat and on foot along the canal. He particularly recommended 'escaping the city' to view the rural idyll.

4. The Barton Aqueduct, engineered by James Brindley for the Bridgewater Canal and completed in 1761. It was demolished in 1894 to make way for the new Manchester Ship Canal.

5. Standedge Tunnel is the longest on the nation's canal network, requiring ventilation shafts through the moorland overhead. Although digging and maintaining it was difficult and dangerous, the 200-year-old tunnel remains open to boats today, after a long period of restoration.

6. Saltaire was one of the best known 'model' communities of the Victorian period, designed to offer good-quality housing and amenities that would be 'improving' to the spiritual and moral life of the local workforce.

7. Broad Quay, Bristol, *c.*1785 – looking towards St Michael's Church.
Trade in the city was second only to London, and the variety of people
and goods depicted here reveals the bustle of trade in Bristol
at the end of the eighteenth century (see page 108).

8. The Caen Hill flight of locks was finished in 1810, at the end of the works on
the Kennet and Avon canal. It is the longest in the country, part of the 29-lock
Devizes system to climb to the plain, and was the last section to be completed.

9. William Smith's geological delineation map was the first of its kind (see page 140). The full title on publication in 1815 was 'A Delineation of the Strata of England and Wales with part of Scotland; exhibiting the collieries and mines, the marshes and fen lands originally overflowed by the sea, and the Varieties of Soil according to the variations in the Substrata, illustrated by the most Descriptive Names by W Smith.'

10 & 11. These photographs show navvies cutting the docks on the Manchester Ship Canal, working with the help of 'steam navvies' as well as horse power.

12. 'Work' by Ford Madox Brown, 1863. Brown admired manual workers and used real navvies as models for this work. The painting is filled with clues to the Victorian attitude to working people, and the virtues of 'honest' work over begging and crime – from the campaigner and Lady Temperance activist to the hawkers and hard-working navvies themselves.

13. Braunston Top Lock, c.1912. Older children were expected to work on boats and the towpath as well as help take care of younger siblings. In a large family, children were often 'borrowed' to help relatives and friends who needed an extra hand or babysitter.

14. A nineteenth-century map of the Birmingham Canal Navigations. By this time, Birmingham was already at the heart of what had become a network to connect with other waterways along rivers and man-made cuts.

15. The King's Norton Junction House, on the Birmingham and Worcester Canal, is today a private residence, but was in the nineteenth century a tollhouse. Here, at this busy point, the canal company could display its all-important charges.

massive scale on slave plantations in the New World meant that the imported raw material was arriving in ever-larger quantities. And that, of course, meant that it fell in price.

Experiments with mixed fibres of cotton and linen now produced a new kind of heavy cloth called fustian. Thanks to its strength in the warp, it worked well under tension and could be woven on a semi-automatic loom. Further innovations like John Kay's 'flying shuttle' allowed the same principle to be applied to cotton in a factory environment, if the right machinery could be developed. The refining of prototype machines, as well as social and economic changes across the land, helped to put everything in place. Manchester's factories were born.

A SKYLINE OF CHIMNEYS

By the mid-1800s automatic machines powered by line shafting and belts had been developed. This meant that a spinning operative did not have to be experienced or knowledgeable about manipulating fibres. A 'hand' in the factory meant just that. In a spinning room in the nineteenth century the role of the worker was mostly to keep a machine supplied with carded, combed fibre and 'doff off' bobbins when they had been filled, replacing them with empty ones. They had to keep machines clean, running and operating at full capacity. The 'self-acting mule' didn't just spin efficiently and cheaply; it had been refined to twist and spin a weight and strength of cotton which could rival the finest handmade artisan product in its countries of origin.

Weaving had to keep up, otherwise, once again, it would represent an inefficient and expensive 'break' in the flow of supply. The inventor Edmund Cartwright, meeting with a group of Manchester merchants, had heard them observe that, once a patent could be sidestepped, any number of men with capital might be tempted to open factories, but they would be hard pressed to find a workforce to complete the process. Cartwright didn't believe that this was impossible; there might not be enough skilled men, but this could be overcome if power could be harnessed.

From northern Cheshire to the towns of Rochdale, Oldham, Burnley and Blackburn, factories opened. The first half of the nineteenth century saw gradual adaptations to the principle of weaving under tension and at speed. Many developments in the dressing of warps and preparing of yarns, along with increases in the number of picks, all helped to make the process faster, more reliable and cheaper. Across the Pennines and West Yorkshire, looms were built for the manufacture of all clothing types in various methods thereafter known as the 'Lancashire Loom', the 'Tappet' or 'Northrop', depending on the area they came from or the change in their construction.

Once factories started to crowd the skylines of northern towns their populations grew at an astonishing rate. The demand for the goods had not just caused cotton factories to be built but had boosted the sister industries surrounding them, too. Foundries, mines and engineering firms opened up, as did formalized production of chemicals such as industrial detergents, bleaches and dyes, as well as all the plants to produce the goods and services needed by such a large urban population.

The German travel writer and historian Johann Georg Kohl wrote a memoir of his journey through Manchester and on to the manufacturing towns of West Yorkshire in the mid-1840s. On arriving in Manchester, he noted:

> Never since the world began, is there a town like it, in its outward appearance, its wonderful activity, its mercantile and manufacturing prosperity and in its remarkable moral and political phenomenon.

High praise indeed. But he did temper his praise in consideration of the lot of the workers. He discussed their conditions and habits with numerous business owners at functions during his stay and found that many expressed low opinions of the labouring classes and their futures. Before leaving Manchester, Kohl considered that it

MUST be of the Master's interest that his work people should be well clothed and fed, and should enjoy sufficient leisure and rest to keep in good health. It must be in his true interest that they should possess some amount of education and refinement, by which alone they can be rendered really valuable and efficient.

He had found a minority who shared this opinion and endeavoured to provide 'model' communities or working conditions. But such men were few and far between, and their motives often self-interested, but they were worthy of comment for what was then considered an unusual approach.

WHO WERE THE WORKERS?

When the first factories were built they drew in labour from outside the region, from rural areas of Lancashire and especially those whose trades would be directly threatened by changes in output. While development and expansion was being experienced in financial markets and in manufacturing, the effect of a century of change from 1600 was also being felt in farming. Scientific methods were being used to provide greater yields of arable crops as well as in animal husbandry. The buying up of pockets of land from small freeholdings, too, meant that land was owned by far fewer people and these owners would control the market and the levels of employment.

It had always been the case that some landowners and farmers would employ the rural 'labourer' to till the soil, bring in the harvest and do any other work needed in return for food, clothing and protection as well as a wage. But the change to a wage-driven economy was partly what brought about rural migration to urban industrial centres. A working man sold his labour to farmers; the amount of money he could earn was dictated by the season, the success of the harvest, the amount of competition and the whim of the farmer. He had to provide for his family and had very little security, either in the regularity of wages, or accommodation on someone else's land.

In large agricultural communities, tenants were either willing to depart for town or were being forced to leave the area out of necessity. The traditional gentry, the main employers in an area, would find that, without rents coming in, their estates were expensive to run or were foreclosed on by the banks. So these families, too, began to leave, and agricultural labourers saw the old squirearchy abandon the land to be replaced by those who had made money in the towns and cities.

For centuries, the ties which had bound a community together were loyalty to a lord or master, safety and protection within a village, and a shared approach to justice and the organization of labour. A cottage tenant on manorial land had the right to graze animals, to farm a small area and to engage in a trade or the gathering of firewood. Suddenly, all this was seen as a thing of the past. Consolidation of lands into bigger, more productive farms made it harder for society to continue the way it had done for centuries. A series of acts of enclosure were passed in the seventeenth century, continuing throughout the eighteenth and nineteenth, creating legal rights of individual property ownership of land that had previously been common. Anyone who was seen as an obstacle to intensive farming could easily be evicted and had to look for work – and accommodation – elsewhere.

Wages in the northern manufacturing towns were soon outstripping those in counties further south such as Norfolk, Essex, Oxfordshire and Wiltshire. In areas where artisan crafts had helped families supplement their wages, towns were now taking all the trade. Norfolk relied heavily on farming, but its principal town, Norwich, was a centre for woollen production before it was monopolized by the urban sprawl of the West Yorkshire wool towns such as Leeds, Bradford, Huddersfield and Halifax. For some, moving on was a choice and a chance for a better life. For others, going north was the only option.

A familiar picture painted of workers' lives in the towns by contemporary reporters, artists and campaigners is one of abject misery. While the environment in which most of the workers lived and worked was indeed appalling, some of the new factory workers were able to make the most of their circumstances. Until the reforms of factory standards in the 1830s and 1840s, there were few restrictions in how factories could operate, and a large family could earn steady wages which compared favourably with those earned on the land. Writers describing Manchester as filthy, noisome and offensive could as easily have levelled the same criticism at any pre-industrial rural English village. The traditional Sunday night period drama on television peddles the idea of the small but cosy rural cottage and tight-knit family unit, but this can hardly have been the lot of most of the rural poor.

Those writing about the conditions of industrial Manchester in the early nineteenth century noticed that there were, even within the general working classes, differences of rank depending on background and trade as well as a person's place of origin. Here, as in other northern cities, the 'lowest' parts of the town – the filthiest, most overcrowded and deprived quarters – were inhabited by the largest group of immigrants, the Irish.

THE FIRST LARGE GROUPS of rural Irish had come over to England in the eighteenth century to work as 'navvies' (navigators) on the turnpike roads and the canals which were now being cut to provide a network to move the fruits of mass production to town and port. In the later 1700s, at the peak of canal building, this workforce, in addition to their English counterparts forced from the land, was available for much the same reasons. The population had grown in Ireland, but Irish towns had not built up manufacturing centres outside of Belfast and Dublin, which were small by English standards. Less than one-eighth of the Irish were city dwellers.

In Ireland there was no alternative to farming and production of artisan crafts for most families. Land was owned, in the main, by aristocratic English and Anglo-Irish families, and it was parcelled up into small tenancies, farmed by hundreds of families. In cases where a farmer could afford to rent a larger portion, he might sublet plots to people known as 'cottagers', who occupied an even lower place in the society.

On a small plot, adult children who were not yet in a position to marry could easily become a burden. If there were plenty of hands available, these were the mouths which would be harder to feed and they were best advised to seek work elsewhere. Few of the labouring poor were literate or could even speak English, and yet scores of young men left home every year to go 'a-roving', looking for any type of paid work.

'Roving' is a word that describes the movement of prepared textile fibres to be spun into yarn, as they drop down and are twisted together when hand-spun. To 'rove out' was to go away to make something of yourself. The expression came into common use to describe anyone seeking a living away from their village, whether they came back again or not.

Irish songs are full of stories about being a 'rover' or 'roving out', and the best-known songs are full of stereotypical references to bad behaviour during this time of freedom. They often mention a sweetheart by whom they have been rejected, or one who is waiting for them to prove themselves and set up together back home in the Emerald Isle.

> *Me name it is O'Hara, I was twenty in the fall,*
> *There's me Brother Kevin, and we're not alike at all.*
> *I'll never be a bank clerk, no wheat nor barley sow,*
> *I'll kiss me Ma at the break of dawn,*
> *And a roving I will go.*
>
> *Sweet Mary was me sunshine, sweet Mary was so true,*
> *Sweet Mary dug me heart out and she cut it right in two.*
> *Now her voice is callin', as pure as fallin' snow,*
> *O'Hara stop your bawling, for a rovin' you must go.*
>
> *A roving I will go, O I'm off to seek me fortune,*
> *I'll dig for gold by day and then by night, Sor I'll*
> * be courtin'.*
>
> ('A roving', Irish traditional folk song)

The main ambition of these young men was to get out of Ireland and 'make a fortune', if not in the 'Greenfields of Amerikay' then in England. In the early days, the songs and stories mostly focus on making money and coming back to Ireland to settle on land of their own, with their own Mary or Peggy at their sides.

The Irishmen who crossed the water to work on the canals were in many ways the ideal workforce. They were strong, accustomed to working in all weathers and living in tough conditions, and used to the hard physical labour of digging and removing stones from the land for growing wheat and potatoes which formed the staple diet. These men, with the Scottish and Cornish rural poor, were not only robust but they were mobile. Relying on a local labour force to dig a canal usually meant that at peak agricultural periods such as harvest-time or lambing, the men on the cut would disappear. Itinerant labourers, far from home, were more reliable and would generally stay as long as there was paid work before moving on to the next 'diggings'. The expression 'living in digs' is slang for somewhere temporary to stay and comes from this experience of a mobile workforce.

While there were canal labourers from near and far working together, the Irish navvies lodged in the public image because of their numbers and their 'separateness'. They spoke another language, had a particular cultural identity, different religious practices (80 per cent were Roman Catholic) and,

This cartoon, from *Punch* in 1865, relates to the arrival of navvies in Oxford to work on the Great Western Railway. The thought of being overrun by the working classes, complete with all their vices, is alarming – even if they have money to spend.

most importantly, were not bound by family or community in England. If they wanted to behave badly, there wasn't much to stop them. Any settled community would be put out by the sudden appearance of hundreds of young, unattached men living in makeshift camps, working all day and, so it was said, drinking all night.

While that may be the stereotypical image of the Irish navvy, it is true that some spent a good portion of their wages 'in drink'. Cartoons and broadsheet songs lambast the navvy as drunk, lazy, stupid and a 'show-off' or a 'flash'. They came, within a very short time, to be a recognizable figure on stage because of the clothes they wore and the way they behaved. There are references in newspapers as well as in verse to men in corduroy breeches and leather tunics with brightly coloured headgear, as well as with a shovel or wheelbarrow.

A theatre audience knew that as soon as such a figure appeared on the stage he would speak with a ridiculous, laboured West of Ireland accent and drink or fight everything in sight. Part of the construction of this stereotype came from the fact that most navvies were relatively well paid at around two shillings a day. This 'danger money' reflected the tough nature of the work and the need to hold on to reliable men. For most of the labourers such money would have been more than they'd ever seen. It was there to be spent. Many of them invested in 'flash gear', to mark their success as well as to stand out from a crowd. It was important to maintain an identity when everything else that could provide one had been removed. Drinking, smoking and spending time with 'easy' company would also quickly deplete earnings. Unless a man was very disciplined and careful about keeping his earnings safe, he might find himself no better off at the end of a job than he was at the beginning.

Part of the problem was that cash for wages proved a difficulty for the companies digging canal cuts. In rural areas where goods were often paid for and settled on account, there was not enough cash to pay all the wages at once. Plenty of navvies ended up receiving wages in arrears, and they might come in the form of a token or note to be redeemed at high interest or at a 'Tommy shop' where goods might be overpriced and of inferior quality. In Lancashire, poor quality or dreary food is still sometimes referred to as 'Tommy'.

A worker's experience would depend on the standard of the gangmaster he worked for. Masters were usually subcontractors who hired small groups of men and some paid a basic wage with rewards for 'good work' or being ahead of schedule, as well as imposing fines for bad behaviour and for lost or broken equipment that might cause slowing down or stoppage of work.

The organization of the diggers often fell to subcontractors who would hire out gangs of men and pay them accordingly. In some cases, a group with a good reputation might be able to negotiate better rates of pay, and through an early form of 'combination' form a 'butty gang' (a crew of friends or acquaintances agreeing to work together) who could ensure they had men who could read and write as well as speak up eloquently for them. These enlightened groups could capitalize and work their way out of poverty, but most would remain at the bottom level.

The Irish in general tended not to turn to factory work en masse when they arrived: they were unused to collective labour under managers or to working set hours. They tended to continue in the type of work they had originally sought – digging and shifting – with women more likely to work in service, laundry work or in hawking goods.

The later waves of immigrants, once settled, were more likely to stay. There was nothing for them to return to, and the establishment of communities meant that a man's kin were also likely to follow him in his trade. Some of the descendants of these emergency immigrants would be those who helped build the Manchester Ship Canal.

THE 'BIG DITCH'

The North West and Lancashire was a region rich in canals, boasting some of the most ground-breaking feats of engineering in the story of the waterways. These canals linked the manufacturing hubs and provided a route to the places where products would be brought for sale to the domestic market, or removed to the ports for export overseas. The original Bridgewater Canal, running from Castlefield to Runcorn, was cut for the Duke of Bridgewater to move his coal from Worsley to Manchester. The Leeds and Liverpool Canal had branches to Leigh and Rufford in north Lancashire. The Rochdale Canal ran from the centre of Manchester through a junction with the Bridgewater, over the Pennine hills through Hebden Bridge to Halifax, some of which is parallel to the modern M60 motorway. The Ashton Canal ran from the lower city centre to join the Huddersfield Narrow. The Peak Forest Canal, originally counted as part of Stockport, ran through what is now Greater Manchester from Dukinfield in Hyde, New Mills and Marple, to Whaley Mill in Derbyshire.

In the case of Manchester and its neighbouring industrial towns, especially those relying on cotton textiles, exports were not the only concern. Importing raw product was costly, and textile magnates felt they were not getting good deals on shipping because they were being held to ransom under monopoly through the port of Liverpool.

Even before the influential Bridgewater Canal, the success of which helped to prompt a flood of investment, the idea for a ship canal had been discussed in Manchester. The existing river navigation of the Mersey and Irwell could only accommodate light coasting boats. This meant unloading vast cargoes at Liverpool, paying for warehousing and dock work, and then hiring numerous craft for the journey north. Linking canals had been built from the North West to Merseyside, yet Liverpool retained the right to charge at docks outside of the city, such as at Warrington on the Bridgewater.

The rates charged throughout the nineteenth century were particularly high because those who controlled them were aware that use of other port cities by canal routes was impractical. This represented a stranglehold over business with world markets in the region, and Manchester spent a hundred years trying to find a way round it. One idea was to build a canal to the River Dee, which was out of Liverpool's jurisdiction, but the marshes around Cheshire meant that it would simply have been impossible to keep such a route cleared and maintained.

One plan in the early nineteenth century was for a canal that would allow the ocean-going ships of the time to pass. At first, letters to newspapers put the case for a canal to link to the sea, but such a plan was roundly disputed and ridiculed by the city of Liverpool. Those with a vested interest in maintaining the status quo could always be relied on to be hostile, and the continued arguments for and against helped to develop a sense of rivalry between cities that were neighbours but rarely easy bedfellows. The first attempts to look at building prompted comedic and sometimes aggressive backbiting in newspapers and popular songs between Manchester and Liverpool.

In February 1825, the *Liverpool Mercury* reacted to a proposal for a bill through Parliament:

> *Oh ye lords of the loom, pray avert us our doom,*
> *We humbly beseech on our knees;*
> *We do not complain if you drink your champagne,*
> *But leave us our port, if you please.*
>
> *Sweet squires of the shuttle, as ye guzzle and guttle,*
> *Have some bowels for poor Liverpool.*
> *Your great ship canal will produce a cabal,*
> *Then stick to the jenny and mule.*
>
> *Your sea-scheme abandon, for rail-roads the land on.*
> *And to save us from utter perdition,*
> *Cut your throats if you like, but don't cut the dike,*
> *And this is our humble petition.*

Although a bill was not passed, the Mersey and Irwell Company asked for a survey to be made to improve the navigation in order to take such vessels. A number of engineers were consulted in the first half of the century, among them John Rennie, who would be instrumental in the building of the

Kennet and Avon Canal in the south of England. But, despite the deepening of the Irwell and Weaver to take larger craft, none became a ship canal.

Not all opposition came from Liverpool; Mancunians themselves joked about overstretching the city's resources in building a 'white elephant' which might harm rather than help trade. Wilmot Henry Jones, a printer on Market Street close to the Victoria Railway Station, distributed broadsheets which both praised and criticized the venture.

> *Your Mayor and Councillors leave in the stocks,*
> *Deepen your rivers and dig out your docks,*
> *Import your own cargoes close up to your doors,*
> *And warehouse and bond upon Manchester's floors.*
> *Your home and your foreign trade shall increase,*
> *And yours be the quarter of commerce and peace.*
>
> ('Manchester as it might be: 1845')

The idea never went away, but it was widely felt that a ship canal would be necessary, albeit expensive compared to the expansion of the railways in the 1840s and 1850s. By the 1870s it was clear that, despite the extensive network of rail, passenger transport was a focus and Liverpool still controlled access to world markets because even using rail from another port remained prohibitively expensive.

The growing rail interests around the region did, however, play a pivotal role in getting the Manchester Ship Canal built. By the second half of the nineteenth century, railway companies had bought up canal property and carrying concerns so that they might have a monopoly. In 1872, one – the Bridgewater Navigation Company – was formed to control the waterway and its carriage.

A couple of years on, one Mr George Hicks, passing the adjoining River Mersey estuary, noticed that barges were marooned in mud as a result of neglect, and decided that a perfectly serviceable waterway could be redeveloped. He wrote to the *Manchester Guardian* to propose that investment be found to improve by expansion. He also approached the Manchester Chamber of Commerce. It was going to take expert opinion to get local businessmen and councillors to support a project which would be very expensive, so Hicks contacted an engineer named Hamilton Fulton, who had recently worked on improvement projects, asking for initial reports that might encourage more people to get behind the scheme. Fulton began surveying the area and its geographical make-up, with the help of a Manchester University scholar named Boyd Dawkins.

So began a process of persuasion. The first meeting was set up in 1882 in the home of a prominent engineer-industrialist named Daniel Adamson. Adamson had established a boiler-making business in the Hyde area of Manchester and, like many other such businessmen, had purchased a grand Gothic mansion house. The Towers, situated in the leafy suburb of Didsbury, lay close to the old coaching inns which had once provided a convenient stopping-off place on the turnpike road south, as well as the path of the River Mersey. This enormous and rather impractical building later became known as the Shirley Textile Institute, a meeting place and centre research into cotton and man-made fibres in its last years. Today, only the lodge can be seen from Wilmslow Road, as the main house lies behind a modern business park and popular cricket club.

At this first influential meeting, Dawkins and Fulton's work was discussed. Their results persuaded those attending the meeting to ask for cost breakdowns to be put together by Fulton and another engineer, Edward Leader Williams, who had worked on the Bridgewater and Weaver navigations.

The men proposed different approaches to construction, with one option being a tidal canal without locks, which was to cost around £5 million. The other idea, put forward by Leader Williams, was for the inclusion of locks, until meeting a tidal range at Warrington and making good use of the geological nature of the land to be cut. With concern about maintenance and the likelihood of silting as well as uncertainty as to the cost of levelling the length of the planned route, the interested parties sought a second opinion from a consultant engineer named Abernathy and formed a committee. They eventually opted for Leader Williams' plans and began fundraising to get the project off the ground while preparing a bill to be put before Parliament.

There were a number of setbacks. Opponents with vested interests in the railways argued that a new canal would take their trade. The railways and the Merseyside Dock complained

An illustration of the proposed docks at Manchester, from the *Illustrated News* in 1883. The Manchester Nine Docks, which originally covered parts of Manchester, Salford and Stretford as the Port of Manchester, opened to trade just short of a hundred years before formal closure. It is now the site of a large retail, leisure and commercial complex, including Media City.

and prevented bills being passed. Different routes and methods were suggested, but the committee pushed on determinedly.

> With regard to the canal itself, I think a greatly improved waterway between Manchester and Liverpool is bound to be made, and that it would be a great blessing to Manchester and no damage to Liverpool. I am one of those who has never had any jealousy whatever on the question of competition between water and rail. I believe there is a trade for the water and a trade for the rail.
>
> (Sir Edward Watkins, 24 January 1883)

After much wrangling, the bill for an altered project was eventually passed in the Commons and the Lords. The cut was going to have to get through substantial rock along the route, and there were some doubts as to its depth. When it was finished, a small labour force was kept on to excavate further and allow deeper hulled vessels to pass. The canal avoided the Mersey estuary as requested, but, as a result, was longer than originally planned.

The promoters of the MSC had to buy out the Bridgewater Canal as well as the Mersey and Irwell, which led to the demolition of the magnificent aqueduct built by James Brindley a century earlier. Nobody had believed then that such a piece of engineering would ever see the light of day and, at the time of its destruction, naysayers were voicing the same doubts about the MSC. The scheme was going to cost more than £6 million and the money spent at the start of the digging had already amounted to a personal fortune. If financial backers couldn't be found quickly to cover the additional costs, the whole struggle would be for nothing.

By 1887, when the money was being called for, Daniel Adamson was heading up the committee, but he was a businessman not a stockbroker. The standards of living for working people were improving slowly in the second half of the century, but the textile trade and others of its ilk had seen periods of bust as well as boom and manual workers' wages were uncertain. Any extra money which could be earned was generally kept for those expenses that wages could not cover, such as medical treatment and even, for a small number, the establishment of a private mortgage or pension fund. Adamson assumed that the canal would be so exciting to the ordinary people of Manchester that they would flock to buy cheap shares. He offered his own workpeople at Dukinfield and Hyde the chance to work overtime in order to afford 'shilling shares' to try to raise £2 million to buy the existing canals. He hoped to raise the rest from the banks. He was disappointed on every count.

Adamson had grown up poor in the North East, and for some he represented the archetypal Victorian moral hero, an example of what could happen when a man came to an industrial heartland and made his fortune through personal dynamism and hard work. His addresses to Parliament in support of the MSC bill show him to be a tenacious, outspoken and strident character; in fact, he was often accused of being stubborn and unwilling to compromise or adapt, even in the face of financial pressures. It was felt among the directors that having a more measured voice 'in charge' would be more acceptable to supporters. Ironically, then, Adamson's 'working man' credentials were considered more a liability than a bonus. But it was largely his early campaigning and personal enthusiasm for the work which ensured that a competent technical team was ready to begin.

To get his project to work – and to attract the share sale prices needed – Adamson accepted that it would have to be under another man's leadership. He relinquished the chair, but remained on the board. Lord Egerton of Tatton Hall in Cheshire took his place and in November 1887 things had moved on sufficiently for the directors of the Manchester Ship Canal Company to meet at Eastham on Merseyside. There they announced the beginning of the work, and held a ceremonial cutting of the 'first sod'.

Mr J. A. Walker, the contractor together with his representative Mr Topham and other assistants, was also present – an ordinary navvy's spade having been provided by the Chairman, Lord Egerton cut the first sod of the undertaking in the centre of the site of the entrance locks.

The Deputy Chairman cut the second sod, followed by the other directors present, who filled an ordinary navvy's barrow, which was wheeled and tipped by Mr E. Leader Williams.

(Minutes of the Board of Directors Meeting of the Manchester Ship Canal Company, 11 November 1887, Manchester Central Library Special Collections)

George Hicks, the Mancunian campaigner who had, in effect, started the ball rolling, was listed among these men by the *Manchester Guardian*, the newspaper to which he had first appealed. He must have felt a certain amount of pride as well as trepidation, as the monumental undertaking was publically committed to.

A RADICAL PLAN

Thomas Andrew Walker was the principal contractor who would supervise the construction work, which was to be undertaken in sections. He was experienced in underground railway cuttings for the transport network in London, and had built the Severn Tunnel which ran under the river. This background and his training as a professional engineer gave him the specialist knowledge with which to approach the exceptionally deep cut and shore up the banks of the excavation.

The cutting work was to be divided into eight sections under Edward Leader Williams; Walker then subcontracted separate engineers and assistants for each of these sections. They could hire their own crews, but would all answer to him. Such an arrangement would inevitably lead to competition between crews, which Walker believed could be put to good effect. This measure had the added advantage of preventing the whole workforce from being able to form a union easily in order to press for better pay and conditions. Crews worked the sections in tandem, which meant that the work could proceed faster and that resources would be more evenly shared. The problem was that so many men couldn't be housed adequately on site at the same time. There was thus great pressure on existing local housing, and it quickly became clear in the way accommodation was provided that the navvies didn't have an equal experience. Depending on whether or not a man was subcontracted, and how his team was organised, he might be offered preferential company digs, or have to find his own at inflated prices.

When Adamson had hailed the coming of the MSC and the jobs it would bring, he had been optimistic that his project would do more than operate a 'trickle-down economy effect'. He hoped that a richer Manchester would in turn make all its citizens richer, by curing some of the distress caused by bust in the textile and manufacturing plants.

The socialist paper *Commonweal* claimed that Adamson was mistaken in his opinions and that there was 'no sign of a decrease in the numbers of unemployed. On the contrary, the numbers of unemployed are being added to daily.' Although the reporters had an agenda of their own, it was true that not all comers would be able to get regular navvying work.

Many unemployed men turned up to the works from 1888 onwards, only to find that Walker 'wasn't hiring'. Although men were taken on, Walker was aware that employing people on a short-term emergency basis, or hiring farmhands who would return to the land at peak periods, was not good for business. He had been offered bonus payments for each section completed ahead of schedule, and in order to get the best he preferred to hire professional gangers and their men. These were mostly the crews who followed him from his last project. They were the 'professional' navvies.

A number of sources talked of the ship canal navvies as '6ft giants, weighing 14 or 15 stone'. A *Manchester Guardian* reporter in 1889 wrote that such a labourer could be called a 'magnificent engine of labour'. These magnificent men were very different from the average urban unemployed. They had spent years on the cut and were nearly all from agricultural backgrounds. Not only were these 'super navvies' fitter and stronger, and more likely to get hired, they were rewarded with better pay and conditions as well. Like the teams of workers 150 years before, crews were able to benefit from the use of equipment to help with the cutting and lifting of material and the placing of supports. Steam cranes and mechanical bucket excavators were used, but that didn't mean that men with spades and horses were a thing of the past. In addition to the 100 steam-powered excavators along the cut, there were 16,361 men and boys listed as having been employed on the project. That doesn't mean they were all employed at once – or even continuously – but it none the less represents a colossal workforce.

More notable still was that, despite the scale of the work and all the mechanical equipment and pumps available, they were still working with their hands. The Ship Canal collections at Manchester's Central Library and elsewhere show us men who look very similar to their earlier forebears, with rough clothes, tanned skin and shovel in hand (see Plates 10 and 11).

There had been widespread concern that all the machinery (which needed very small teams to operate it) would put men out of work but, as it transpired, actually getting the machines on site and stopping them falling into the cut was difficult in itself. The excavators were only adept at shifting large tonnages of loose soil, not rock. Walker had observed that although the diggers could move 2000 tons of loose soil in good conditions, on average the amount removed was more like 700 tons. If it was wet and the ground became boggy, or the cut was full of rocks, it fell to men with shovels, picks and wheelbarrows. Just as it had over a century before.

Horses – 196 of them – were also used along the diggings, harnessed to winches to pull up heavy barrows full of rock and earth, and guided by the labourers. Men had to push barrows up steeply planked canal sides to be tipped. They could be winched up by horse power, and some men were able to complete a barrow run very quickly. Although they could be very effective in certain conditions, machines often could not be lowered to the bottom of the cut, because it was simply too deep. Poor conditions or flooding made this sort of work extremely dangerous, further exacerbated by the need to work overtime and shifts at night to get the work completed as fast as possible.

Working long hours at pace in wet weather by poor light (lamps and torches were employed) was partly responsible for the 154 deaths through accident and the 1404 major or serious injuries sustained by the navvies. A resident surgeon named Robert Jones was eventually brought on to the canal in 1889.

Jones, just 31 years old, suddenly had a potential 17,000 patients and hundreds of cases to deal with. There were countless serious injuries, many of which required some degree of amputation, and he had to monitor and treat infectious illnesses in the navvy villages. He established three hospitals – the first hospitals set up solely to address accidents and emergencies – and a chain of first-aid stations along the canal route.

Walker had personally organized dredging and the instructions for the setting of the sluice gates up to the point at which the cut became tidal. He operated in a very methodical manner and ensured that work was well planned and carried out in a timely fashion. Things began to go wrong in 1889 when Walker (aged 60 at the time the bill was passed) died suddenly. Work carried on without him, but not to his regime of what today might be called 'health and safety'. Controls needed to be put in place for a building site employing the population of a small town. And it wasn't just the men, animals and machines working in these built-up areas; the scale of every aspect of the work was immense. The Eastham docks alone, which provided access to the canal (and didn't even act as a regular 'lifting lock') had gates of up to 182 metres made from 'greenheart' exotic hardwood timber, heavier and denser than steel, imported specially from Guyana along with the sugar imports which would bring vital revenues into Manchester once the canal was built.

Cutting of the first 'sods' at Eastham to link through the Mersey Estuary.
The originators sailed from Eastham Ferry, a crossing place from medieval
times, to the site of the works to celebrate the beginning of the project.

Working conditions became intolerable. Alongside the
digging itself came the installation of massive metal siphons
for drainage, the use of heavy lifting equipment and torrential
rain in 1889 and 1890 which caused severe flooding at Trafford
and Thelwall. Frosts and thaws and further floods beset the
works. Costs went up and men were let go. The Thelwall
section's navvies went on strike for higher pay first, and were
unsuccessful. The Manchester Ship Canal Company were
unhappy with the rate of progress and moved to take control
of the contract from Walker's executors to get the job done.
When another strike in 1891 failed, a sense of disillusionment

set in and tensions brewed between the management and the workforce. However difficult the canal was to dig under Walker, it was much worse under the company.

The rulebook for employees laid out what was expected of a company man. It was standard fare for the day. Page five reads:

> The Company may, at any time –
>
> Dismiss without notice or suspend from duty and, after enquiry, dismiss without notice, or suspend from duty as a disciplinary measure an employee of the company for any one or more of the following offences, viz:
>
> Drunkenness
> Disobedience of orders
> Misconduct or negligence
> Absence from duty without leave
>
> Any employee under the above regulation would not be able to claim any wages and any rent owing on a company property could be deduced from any wages which were earned prior.

Walker was praised at the time of his death for having been a 'benevolent Master' in the patriarchal vein of other employers such as Titus Salt of Saltaire and the Cadburys at Bournville. While it was true that he had provided a number of facilities for navvies as well as accommodation, he did so selectively. The *Manchester Guardian* reported on the 'Walker Huts', wooden cabins of superior quality, built at stages along the works to house navvies and their families, so they could stay close to work and not be inconvenienced. A reporter toured one village in March 1888 to inspect what he had imagined would be a filthy shanty town and wrote eagerly that he had been quite mistaken.

The rents were described as high, but the reporter reasoned that the food the men ate was bland and cheap and that they could hardly be badly off as a result. There was access to food delivery wagons from grocers and suppliers when away from shops, as well as provision of religious service in the chapel, Sunday schools and night classes for literacy. But this benevolence was only open to the 'butty gang'. These groups of handpicked men were the ones who got the overtime and all the perks of the job, while the other 'labouring fill' had to find accommodation themselves in lodging houses or private homes. Those men earned less, had the worst work and the least assistance.

Each worker was obliged by Walker to pay a percentage of his salary into an insurance fund. This money was used to fund sick pay for three months at a reduced rate (although not enough to pay the rent) in order that a sick or injured man might be able to resume work upon recovery. Interestingly, although sick pay was not exactly common in Victorian Manchester, the premiums were higher than most people's contributions to 'sick clubs' or pensions, and didn't pay anything out in compensation in the event of a man's death at work, beyond a cheap burial at the local graveyard.

Walker's death elicited enthusiastic eulogies in local newspapers, but one publication printed a scathing assessment of his attitude towards navvies:

> With regard to the wooden villages, the late Mr Walker charged each tenant 10 shilling per week (the MSC Company listed it as 8). It was true that Mr Walker read the bible to those who attended mission hall on Sundays, but most of the navvies needed rest after working day and night in that dark, wet hole, with bad, foul air tainted with naphtha lamps and blasting of dynamite.
>
> At one time, many poor fellows died there [on the Severn Tunnel under Walker], from smallpox. The corpses of these were thrown into brick carts

and taken to the grave like so many dogs. I speak
of things as I find them, and I like to give honour
where honour is due.

These strident words were printed in a short-lived magazine
called the *Navvy's and Labourer's Guide*. It was produced by the
Navvies, Bricklayers and General Labourers Union in 1889.

COMBINE OR STARVE

The union was the brainchild of a socialist journalist, Leonard
Hall, and a canal labourer, John Ward. Hall worked at the
Eccles Advertiser and lived in the district, along with scores
of the poorer 'low-class' navvies. He was also a reporter
and 'Manchester correspondent' for a socialist newspaper
called *Justice*.

Ward was, like many others, a former agricultural labourer
(in Surrey), and, having taken the route of self-education,
was determined to improve the lives of the working poor
through access to education and awakening them to social
injustice through politicization. Ward had been a navvy since
working on the canals as an assistant at the age of 12. By the
time he came to the MSC he had amassed a fair amount of
experience, not just in canal building but in world affairs and

politics. Years before coming to Manchester, Ward had joined a socialist party called the Social Democratic Federation, and he stood for election before the Ship Canal was finished. The party was dogged by fallings out and splits to both right and left, and in the end his route to political office would come through the Liberal Party.

Ward became the President of the new union, and quickly moved to London in order to recruit more members. Although the cause had a number of branches in Greater Manchester and, by 1890, some 3000 members in Oldham, Runcorn, Warrington, Preston and Blackburn, navvies on the MSC alone weren't going to provide adequate membership. The union reps worked on attracting other groups of workers who were at risk of exploitation because of the disorganized traditions of their industries.

John Ward sent word back to Manchester that, when he had raised the issue of the horrific levels of accidents on the MSC, the prevailing attitude of the powers that be towards the workers was one of apathy:

> Mr Cunningham Grahame, MP, the best and only friend of Labour as yet in parliament, asked for a return on accidents occurred to labourers on the Manchester Ship Canal. Old Lady Matthews, the Home Secretary 'regretted' that he did not have a

thing to say about him and did not mean to have
… just so.

To publish all the 'accidents' that lie at the foot
of capitalist greed and indifference might shock
the nervous system of the people who sent to
Parliament such wire worked puppets as Matthews
or his predecessor Harcourt, for that matter.

In 1891, the Conservative Home Secretary Henry Matthews
was reeling from a backlash of public opinion after the
embarrassing failure of the police to successfully conclude
the hunt for Jack the Ripper. This, too, was fodder for the
socialist newspapers and the argument that the landed and
privileged – as well as the business classes – were prepared to
sacrifice the working classes to just about any fate so long as
they were kept from rising up. It didn't help that Matthews
had made a number of public gaffes about child labour and
working-class education. He said that half-time mill-working
children – those who attended school for part of the day and
worked the rest – learned more by working than they would if
they were at school full time, and that such a background was
compatible with the natural 'technical education', which was
what a working-class child needed.

The *Navvy's Guide* prompted its readers and union members
to question established opinion and to look for better conditions

as well as the education of younger generations as the only way out of stagnation and abuse within the class system.

In the days of the formation of the navvies' union, however, it was felt that if only men would join, they would be able to fight for better conditions and rights in the same way that factory, mine and railway workers could. There was still a strong traditionalist attitude to 'the power of combination'. William Fairbairn of Fairbairn and Lillie (engineers and steam-crane builders) of Manchester had remarked to a newspaperman in the 1850s that, when faced by possible industrial action, he approached the discontented among his workforce by collecting those who had the most education and persuading them in a 'friendly and sensible way' until they '[saw] the folly of their proceedings, and [acted] as checks upon the turbulence and stupidity of the rest'. Unsurprisingly, Fairbairn was also a supporter of the Ship Canal and heralded not improvement for the city's poor but the 'epoch of such commercial magnitude'.

The push for combination came at a time when more strikes were taking place than ever before. Not all of them were successful, but although the failures were more heavily publicized, those which achieved improvement in pay or conditions for workers were held up as shining examples of what might be achieved. The Navvies, Bricklayers and General Labourers Union oversaw a number of strikes based on wage cuts which were ultimately unsuccessful. After Walker's death, the night overtime rate was cut under the leadership of the Manchester Ship Canal Company, partly due to problems with weather and overspending. Cutting the night rate meant that navvies were no longer getting danger money. The work was even more difficult and dangerous due to increased slippages and accidents caused by poor weather. Gradually, relations between the company and the crews worsened. A letter to the directors in the summer of 1891 was written from 'Salford Comrade' and addressed:

> To a certain swag-bellied bummer on the ship canal.

> You may clothe a hog in broadcloth, but when he speaks, you are reminded of the grunts at the swill tubs.

The union was relatively short-lived, as was its publication, which only managed eight editions. The rhetoric was inflammatory even for socialist publications, and few organizations wanted to be associated with it or its members.

In a period of uncertainty, so many striking workers had been forced to capitulate that many opted out of the fledgling unions altogether. Navvies were particularly vulnerable to dropping out because of the nature of their work. The union lost members to other organizations as and when navvies took on other work, and eventually, in 1929, the navvies' union amalgamated into the Transport and General Workers' Union.

Having given up leadership of the navvies' union in the 1890s to campaign for political office, John Ward understood the way politics worked. He saw that poor levels of education could be used as an excuse to exclude working-class people from decision making. He urged the labour force and those who would eventually be his voters to educate themselves in order to avoid being waylaid by such tactics. By the time of his election, the socialist rhetoric had been toned down considerably:

> The class WAR leaves no room for invidious distinctions, craft jealousies, or unorganised forces. The workers of each and every occupation must combine or STARVE. The trade unions must federate or DIE. John Ward – *Navvy's Guide*, January 1891.

Ward had, by the time the Ship Canal was completed in 1894, begun to believe that the only way he could engineer change was from the inside as an MP. When the Labour Party was formed in 1906, Ward stood for election, but he disagreed with the party's constitution and refused to sign up to it. He became MP for Stoke-on-Trent as a 'liblab', a candidate maintained by a trade union and supported by a local liberal association. Gradually, Ward began to steer away from the left, rejecting the tenets of socialism altogether after witnessing the actions of the Bolshevik Army and the condition of the Russian people during his posting in Russia during the First World War.

John Ward put his position in life down to his early years as a navvy. He had begun to follow the public speeches and writings of men like Robert Blatchford of the *Clarion* newspaper and public addresses by figures such as Keir Hardie as well as other campaigners for what would become the Workers Party or the Independent Labour Party. Although the established political class and business leaders were alarmed at what they saw as a rise in representation by those who might support a revolution, in fact most of the new MPs who attended Parliament represented a more centred view to that of the growing number of socialists and communists on the left wing.

Ward amassed a large library of books, begun in youth with the creation of Everyman's Library of cheap classics such as *Robinson Crusoe*, the first title Ward reckoned to have purchased for fourpence – an hour's wage on the Canal.

> Reading changed the course of my life, let me
> tell you. Twenty years ago, British navvies were
> intellectually the lowest, as they were physically the

finest class in the country. They took absolutely no interest in public affairs, in the mess hut or the canteen you never heard a word of discussion on social or political matters and so, it was books alone that directed my thoughts towards progress and reform.

Today's navvies are among the keenest and most intellectual critics on social and political questions, and I am proud to think that my work amongst them has helped them awaken from the mental torpor in which they were plunged.

In a way, Ward's reminiscences as an elderly man were just as prejudiced as William Fairbairn's views of a generation earlier. Intellectual or not, in most cases the navvy working independently felt that union membership might be enough to prevent him from being able to bring home pay. In a situation where bosses could choose men who were in or out of a union, they would inevitably choose those who were 'free of combination'. The post-Walker years of the Ship Canal's construction were categorized by waves of unemployment as thousands of men were turned off the cut. The truth was, those who couldn't afford to risk the loss of their job didn't, and the nature of the work itself meant that there was a choice either to continue in transitory work without representation or take up formal work elsewhere. Most who could did the latter. Census returns for 1891 show a large number of people listed as 'agricultural labourers' born in Ireland and living in Manchester around Cadishead, Partington and Eccles, close to the Canal but not listed as working as navvies.

THE WONDERS OF THE WATERFRONT

Despite all the setbacks of the early 1890s, the Manchester Ship Canal was opened to traffic on 1 January 1894. A flotilla of 70 ships came through Mode Wheel Lock to be welcomed by the elderly Queen Victoria. Even the previous winter, when the directors of the MSC Company boarded the barge *Snowdrop* to sail from Eastham near Merseyside and inspect the works, there had been no certainty the project would be completed. In fact, it would be some years before it started to earn money. Those working men who had disappointed Adamson so much in the early days had been right to be cautious. The project had cost double the estimated amount, and afterwards was in continuous use for just 80 years.

While the Canal didn't raise the people of Manchester out of poverty in the early twentieth century, it did help to contribute to its sense of optimism for the future of the city's trade and supporting industries. A canal historian of the late

Cartoons in the political magazine *Punch* joked about the notion of
bringing the sea to Manchester, calling it 'Manchester Sur Mer' in
1882. This later cartoon, published after the canal was opened, shows
Manchester being introduced to Neptune by Edward Leader Williams,
Chief Architect of the Ship Canal, in a game of 'follow my Leader'.
If it was possible in Manchester, why not elsewhere?

1970s, writing about the MSC Company, commented that the trade in container shipping and the building of the Trafford Park industrial estate had stimulated Manchester's growth to the point that its big business was becoming something else:

> Pomona Docks have a deserted look, though they are still used ... Just beyond the Trafford Road bridge, the modern docks begin and they are full of life and activity.
>
> (David Owen, *Canals to Manchester*, Manchester University Press, 1977)

By this point in the mid-seventies, most of Britain's traditional manufacturing and heavy industries were in trouble. Changes in demand and lifestyle as well as competition in developing and newly independent Commonwealth countries meant that international shipping was affected. Container shipping had grown in the post-war years but, gradually, parts of the canal became less navigable and harder to maintain for the amounts of revenue coming in. As well as air freight, motorway transport networks were cheap, fast and direct, creating the competition that would eventually cement the Ship Canal's fate.

Once again, towards the close of the twentieth century word spread about the regeneration of the dock and canal and it was hoped that the local area council, the City of Salford, would be able to encourage growth by buying the site. In 1984, a century after its ambitious beginnings, locals were again sceptical that the canal and docks could be made to pay. Work to turn the docks around was slow, but then investment and development on the waterfront mirrored an economic boom in the mid-1990s based on financial and service industry growth. The city centre population soared and wanted to live close by, in 'modern apartments with northern heritage character'. Docks 6, 7, 8 and 9 were built on by the Peel Group and leased to restaurants, bars, shops and the Media City complex.

The Dock Authority Office sitting at the Trafford Road end of the complex remains undeveloped. Coming full circle, the buyers of the site for development of luxury accommodation are LiveMan Properties, a company set up by a new group of Manchester-based businessmen to acquire and capitalize on the industries of service and leisure.

The Ship Canal changed Manchester. From its creation in 1894, the Port of Manchester went on to become the third largest in the country, linking the city to the rest of the world. An efficient transport system enabled Britain to kick-start the Industrial Revolution. The canals – and later the railways – gave the country the motorways of their age and changed the face of rural Britain.

Without an army of anonymous workers it could never have happened.

5

THE FAMILY:
THE EAST MIDLANDS

THE ROUTE OF THE CURRENT Trent and Mersey Canal runs from Derbyshire into Cheshire via the area now known as the Potteries. From there, it links with the Shropshire Union, Caldon and Macclesfield canals, as well as meeting with routes in the Midlands and north Leicestershire. This region became well known during the golden age of canals as a transport centre – today it would be described as a 'gateway zone' or 'hub'. It was a place where single cuts and navigations became a network, and where entire families came to live and work on the water. Men, women and children toiled for long hours, often in dangerous conditions and at huge personal cost.

Why here? The region of Birmingham and its neighbouring towns and cities became established at the end of the eighteenth century as a centre for the manufacturing trades based on locally found natural resources, the basic building blocks of an industrial economy. An industrialist might manufacture goods cheaply and at speed, but he needed cheap raw materials to build factories as well as to produce his goods. The South Staffordshire, Derbyshire, Nottingham and Leicestershire areas were literally dug out for the coal, iron and clay they contained.

The lay of the land gives away the natural resources underfoot. The Derbyshire peaks formed in grit stone with fast-flowing waters were ideal for powering early industrial processes through pumps and wheels. The lower-lying areas below the coalfields of the Midlands provided cities such as Nottingham with good riverside bases for sister industries to spring up alongside the larger industrial plants. Despite the mechanization of one of the region's traditional industries, framework lace-making and hosiery, Nottingham itself became less well known for its handmade lace and better for its production in scale of manufactured goods and pharmaceuticals (through the chemicals giant Boots), as well as new mass-consumption products like cigarettes.

The focus of industry in the Potteries was in the so-called 'five towns' of Arnold Bennett's novels, though there are actually six: Tunstall, Burslem, Hanley, Stoke-on-Trent, Fenton and Longton. Staffordshire potters had been famous for centuries for producing good-quality ivory as well as coloured clays. Red marl used in earthenware ceramics was the most common type of clay dug, and was used in crockery, tiles and hard-fired bricks for industrial uses such as in ovens. Coarse stoneware was used for making more disposable and cheaper domestic crockery as well as packaging like jam jars. These were often vitrified and salt glazed, appearing very different from the more expensive types of product such as decorative pasteware and the area speciality of bone china. To create a finer, more expensive and desirable product for consumption by the growing middle classes, factories bought in cream clay and used crushed animal bone to improve the brightness of the fired products, as well as making them lightweight and conducive for the hot drinks which had become de rigueur in the 1700s. Clay goods quickly became staple items. Fired vessels kept food and drinks cool and clean and were used to serve the beer and ale that everyone drank, and pottery became the disposable container that most people were able to afford. Some firms began to specialize in sanitary ceramics for institutions such as public bathhouses and hospitals at the same time as developing lines of industrial products for use in insulators, heating systems, and even brake linings and conductors for industrial machinery.

Most of the demand for the region's products was in London and the north. Part of the need for a canal, or at least a navigable river system in the area, was down to the terrain. While the three counties of the East Midlands were blessed with natural resources, the nature of those resources made the land tough to travel across with heavy loads, and very expensive. Creating large brickworks, ironworks and lead mines was all very well, but the goods needed to reach the centres of manufacture and the products needed to reach customers. Londoners wanted coal and domestic ironmongery; northern businesses needed raw products and chemicals to build and expand their industries. Nottingham was able to get its goods moved by using the River Trent. The Trent was navigable, with the added bonus of smaller linking rivers – the Idle and the Derwent – which had been 'improved' in the early eighteenth century.

Nottingham's boundaries were growing and it needed to make the most of the smaller canals which were built during the 'boom' of the eighteenth century, such as the Cromford, Derby and Chesterfield, as well as other later cuts following on from the development of the Erewash Canal. A developing network in the 1790s would make it possible to move from one place to another without too much difficulty. On leaving the Potteries, investors and users would find that this small area was a regular haunt of the people who worked on the boats.

At the start of the industrial period, however, the area around Burslem and Stoke-on-Trent was remote – while not far from the growing centres of population, it was surrounded by undeveloped countryside. This made it difficult to transport fragile goods by roadway without additional cost, or worse, major losses.

This was a problem that one local man was determined to solve.

THE INDUSTRIALIST

Josiah Wedgwood was born into a family of Burslem potters and tried experimenting with slipware and mixes of clay for firing, to produce ceramics with decorative effects as well as strong and robust pieces which would break less easily.

He went into business for himself after being apprenticed to work for his brother Thomas at the Churchyard Works, just at the point when the pottery towns were experiencing boom and expansion. Starting in 1759, at the age of 29, with a factory called Ivy House, which he rented from his retiring uncles, he struck up a number of partnerships and was soon doing well enough to purpose-build a large works called Etruria. The name of the factory was taken from ceramics based on classical styles made popular by Wedgwood. The Mediterranean Ancient World ceramics were believed at the time to be Etruscan in origin. In fact, on the day of opening, a commission was made in blackware of a vase with classical scenes, detailing the new works and bearing the legend *Artes Etruriae Renascuntur* ('the Art of Etruria Reborn'). The new works was opened two years after Wedgwood established a partnership in 1767 with Thomas Bentley of Derbyshire, who had opened a trading business in Liverpool. Wedgwood used Bentley to communicate with colleagues and clients and establish further new ventures. The men kept in touch frequently to discuss business affairs as well as family, friends and ideas.

When Wedgwood's firm produced its 'Portland vase' – a renowned copy in jasperware of an object of antiquity – and began to fulfil commissions for Queen Charlotte, its products became increasingly desirable. It was especially important to Wedgwood to develop a viable method of transportation for his wares, and not only for his London showrooms; Wedgwood looked at the reduction of cost and ease of carriage in canals to expand into world markets, too. Having been interested in canal schemes in the area for some years, Josiah met with James Brindley, the engineer of the Bridgewater Canal in Manchester, at an inn called the Leopard at Burslem to discuss the creation of a major new canal. This canal, when completed, would link up with others to create what Brindley hoped would be the heart of a waterway network, with branches veering off from the Trent and Mersey 'grand trunk' to towns from Leicester and Nottingham up to the salt-producing Cheshire marshes. The plan was to take goods as far as Liverpool and Hull (the principal ports), and would take 11 years to complete. Brindley didn't complete the Trent and

Mersey, however. After his death in 1772, his brother-in-law, Hugh Henshall, was to see the project through.

In order to avoid difficult areas and multiple locks, the route was diverted, making it longer than had originally been planned. Digging tunnels could not be avoided, however, and the tunnel at Harecastle, just above the pottery towns before the junction with the Macclesfield Canal, proved especially problematic. The land purchasing for the deviations was expensive and the original Brindley tunnel was narrow; so narrow that only one boat could be legged through it. Boats couldn't be too heavily laden and the time taken to pass through it was more than two hours in most cases. It prompted Thomas Telford to bore a second, wider tunnel to the left of the original, between Tunstall and Kidsgrove. This was originally used as a double tunnel to allow boats to pass each other, but Telford's towpath in the new tunnel became submerged by subsidence and, once again, crews were forced to pass by turn.

The complex structure of the canals which serve the East Midlands, and the fact that the area features so much traffic in so many directions – almost like a spider's web in the centre of the country – meant that it was bound to become an area where those who worked on the canals would congregate. These workers would still be a part of that landscape well into the twentieth century.

LIFE ON THE CANALS

Once the early canals were dug, they had to be navigated by men with some experience of managing watercraft. The rivers and earlier natural navigations had been traversed by small coracles, rafts and barges for centuries, and men could be found around any important waterway to crew barges and narrow boats for carrying companies, who would charge merchants and producers per ton over set distances.

Where there were only one or two canals, cut over short distances, such as the Bridgewater from Worsley Mines to nearby Manchester, this would simply require daily crews to transport. These men could live locally and their families undertake different work, living close to the cut for convenience. Once the network began to expand, however, this became more difficult. A long and extended waterway such as the Trent and Mersey would involve not just hours, but days or weeks of moving goods. It became increasingly difficult for men to maintain a family in this way, not least because of growing amounts of legislation detailing the ways a narrow boat could or should be crewed.

Most boatmen worked for a carrying company or a boss, who owned the boat and who contracted the captain to work a particular route or take jobs on. Any other crew members were subcontracted by the captain, and were usually members of his family or relatives of friends. Early canal rules and by-laws stated that, because of accidents involving boats too lightly crewed, a narrow boat should always have two crewmen aboard to operate locks and maintain the craft, and some organizations demanded three.

Most crews in the days before motor engines relied on the extra power of horses to tow the boats along, taking them over adjoining ground on approaching tunnels without paths. Although a safe way to transport fragile goods in bulk, the going was slow, and the knock-on effect for a boatman was that he often had tight schedules to meet to avoid his pay being docked.

As the population expanded and competition from other lines and from the railway network came into play, canal companies were forced to reduce their charges. This meant lower wages for the canal crews, forcing many boatmen to take their families out of their rural villages and create permanent homes on board. This was especially true for the Trent and Mersey line, where the competition in the heavily built-up and industrial Midlands area was strongest. The line varied in width, and because of tight 'pinches' to pass boats as well as work to load and unload or repair, a bigger crew was needed to turn boats around quickly.

The inclined plane at Foxton was eventually used to try to reduce pressure on these very narrow locks. As Foxton

Locks was a 'long lock', it took a considerable time to pass and involved heavy work. Any delay would be detrimental to the swift carriage of essential goods such as coal and iron; that is part of the reason why this particular network and its canal community remained as a coal route until the mid-twentieth century. A wife and older child counted as part of the necessary three-man crew, adhering to canal regulations, and would not need to be paid an extra wage. Any man who took his family out of their settled community for a life on the water could dramatically slash his costs. Rent didn't have to be paid, and members of the family could all contribute to earning a living. The children could be apprenticed when old enough. One positive factor was that a family could spend considerably more time together than their counterparts in Nottingham or Stoke-on-Trent, who would have to go to work in factories or attend school separately. Family life on board continued until after the Second World War in the East Midlands, because of the special nature of the lines. Here, families knew each other and established connections and friendships through businesses and marriage as well as 'boatman' villages.

There were indeed difficulties and dangers to life on the canals – it was hard and heavy work, as boatpeople were paid by the weight of the cargo they carried. But it was also true that a life apart represented an element of freedom in a very closed society during the nineteenth century. Canal families did not have to answer to the authorities; living standards and legislation were rarely imposed upon them. In fact, their lives were difficult to record effectively at all: a life on the move meant that canal people were often left out of censuses and lacked official documentation such as marriage and birth certificates.

However, that doesn't mean canal families had no sense of community. Along major routes, there were stopping places such as Stoke Bruerne and Braunston (see Plate 13) in Northamptonshire – considered by many the boatmen's 'spiritual home' – where crews had to wait for a chance to pass or hole up during a stoppage. In spots like these, communities established meeting places, favourite pubs and services aimed at boatmen. Bearing in mind low levels of literacy and a lack of a fixed address, people who needed to send a message would do so at one of these 'hubs', knowing that the person they needed to contact would arrive there sooner or later. They became places to shop, to hold celebrations and to find jobbing work when necessary, helping to create a counterculture of 'waterway villages'.

These floating communities had become firmly established by the mid-1800s and were soon under attack from Victorian writers and political campaigners as representative of a morally reprehensible way of life. The most readily accepted idea of a boatman's life was based less on the work he did than the accommodation he lived in.

The *Illustrated London News* for 10 October 1874 described for its readers, with the help of engravings of the inside of a boat cabin, a 'floating home, under circumstances too often of much discomfort'. The reporter made clear that these were 'not gypsies', although their boats were often colourfully painted and decorated with floral motifs. The distinction was made in this case because, for the journalist, those who worked for a carrying company, especially the large established groups like Pickford's or Fellows, Morton and Clayton, were more respectable.

Since Victorian journalists tended to paint a rather romantic picture of rural existence, one which echoed popular sentiment and respect for cleanliness, education and sobriety, their descriptions of canal life never quite tell the whole story. Conditions aboard boats varied enormously depending on the financial situation of the family and even the goods they were carrying. However house-proud a boatman's wife might be, it was practically impossible to keep such a small space clean – the average cabin was around 7 x 5 feet, an extremely cramped space in which to eat and sleep. Facilities were limited, which meant that most of the family's time was spent outdoors, on the boat or towpath so that cooking and cleaning could be done inside.

The canals themselves were heavily polluted and dangerous and very few canal dwellers would swim in them. Filthy water was always a hazard. Factories, mills and houses all discharged dirty water into canals along with boaters emptying their chamber pots. Diseases like typhoid and cholera were rife – in the 1830s, 70 cases of cholera and 19 deaths were recorded in Braunston alone. In conditions like these, children were particularly vulnerable.

THE DESERVING POOR

Along the line of the Trent and Mersey in the first half of the nineteenth century, entire families engaged in factory work. In any of the major manufacturing centres, young children were employed on full-time hours in menial and manual trades, often for low wages and in dangerous conditions. In the pottery towns, Samuel Scrivens wrote a report in 1842 on the employment of factory children in which he drew attention to the high levels of illness and abuse in the child workforce. Most of these children were employed as ceramic 'dippers', coating pots in glazes that exposed them to high levels of non-soluble lead. Other noxious chemicals were used in the industry, and the grinding of flint for adding to clay caused a range of pneumonic complaints which caused permanent lung damage. The nature of 'put out' work might mean that even if a factory owner didn't employ young children and women in the manual labour trades directly, his employees could, by hiring their own teams of assistants. Even when child educational reform finally arrived in the 1860s and 1870s – stipulating that all children had to attend school for a set number of hours per day – there were still thousands of child labourers in the cities. Conditions at home could be equally poor. Cramped and close living conditions, often in accommodation rented from unscrupulous private landlords, could mean that a family had no running water or toilets, and could be affected by overflowing cesspits, vermin and disease. In all the manufacturing trades there were periods of depression when workers would be put on short time or laid off, making survival for large families much more difficult.

By the middle of the century, housing had been 'thrown up' and there were outbreaks of infectious diseases such as cholera, borne from bacteria in filthy water sources and open sewers. Charles Kingsley (author of *The Water Babies*) wrote in his diary in 1849 that poor people, who would have drunk weak beer in the countryside, had no access to clean water:

> London, October 14th
> I was yesterday with Walsh and M. over the cholera district of Bermondsey, and Oh God! What I saw! People having no water to drink, hundreds of them – but the water of the common sewer

A young girl working at the ovens in a brick-making plant, around 1850.
Child labour was heavily employed in the East Midlands to complete
'unskilled' processes and to carry raw materials as well as load goods.
The working conditions for potteries and brickyard children were
considered shocking even by mid-Victorian standards.

which stagnated full of dead fish, cats and dogs, under their windows. At the time the cholera was raging, Walsh saw them throwing untold horrors into the ditch and then dipping out the water and drinking it!

Social commentators were astounded by the permanency of the factory system and the generations living in such conditions. It had become clear that something had to be done to relieve the levels of suffering in urban areas, and legislation was passed to create proper sewerage and lighting as well as to pave roads and clear them of refuse. The 1848 Public Health Act compelled local authorities to set up boards to monitor and legislate against those who would abuse the rules but they were easy to get around, and often the penalties for overcrowding and failing to remove refuse were small. Between 1842 and 1845, reports were written in all the large industrial centres about the state of working conditions as well as the homes in which workers lived. They uniformly despaired of the slum conditions and the long hours, especially those worked by children. People's behaviour and standards of living were then, as now, hugely varied within the same demographics, and many people tried hard to maintain as clean and comfortable a way of living as possible, given their circumstances.

Gradually, the level of scrutiny applied to town dwellers forced a certain amount of change in the hours worked, the ages of the children employed and facilities for the poorest workers. The 'nuisance inspector' and the 'lady visitor' became common sights in towns and cities. Social reformers and missionaries made it their business to record the state of affairs and to try to improve conditions as well as moral attitude in the slums. To the Victorian mind, a group of people living in squalor must by default be less morally sound and further from religion. Indeed, for the majority of poor labourers, the one day off per week was more happily spent in rest (and sometimes in drink) than in church.

The writings of Thomas Malthus, an Anglican clergyman, had a popular following in the early 1800s. In his essay 'The Principle of Population' he argued that the numbers of working-class people would continue to increase beyond the point where they could earn a living or be fed, and that the natural result would be 'idle poor' who should not receive help from local authorities in order that they be discouraged from breeding. The backlash against this opinion came from Nonconformist and humanist voices like William Cobbett and Samuel Taylor Coleridge, and later by other commentators such as Elizabeth Gaskell. But most reformers were campaigning for better conditions for the people who kept production going, and an overwhelming cultural shift was taking place. A more literate and connected population was coming to accept a change in attitude to working people based on the idea of the 'deserving poor'.

Samuel Smiles put into words the Victorian values associated with hard work. He wrote a number of biographies of the 'great men' who he hoped would be an inspiration to the working classes, including one of Josiah Wedgwood in 1894. His 1859 book, *Self-Help*, is sometimes referred to as the 'bible of mid-Victorian liberalism', and its main message was that strength of character and perseverance through hard times, sticking fast to duty and responsible actions, would keep ordinary people out of the gutter:

> Help from without is often enfeebling in its effects, but help from within invariably invigorates. Whatever is done for men or classes, to a certain extent takes away the stimulus and necessity of doing it for themselves; and where men are subjected to over-guidance and over-government, the inevitable tendency is to render them comparatively helpless.

The ambition for the working classes would be that, through hard work, careful spending and avoiding moral dangers such as drunkenness or gambling, a man could improve his life and the future for his children.

Samuel Smiles was the Victorian equivalent of the lifestyle coach.
He became a bestselling author in the 1860s and in later life wrote
numerous biographies of men whom he believed represented his ideology
by 'helping themselves' to work their way out of poverty to greatness.

Smiles and his followers wanted to help the poor, not by getting involved directly, but by providing places such as mechanics institutes and leisure facilities which would open working-class minds to inspiration.

> The common class of day labourers has given us
> Brindley the Engineer, Cook the Navigator and Burns
> the Poet. Masons and Bricklayers can claim Ben
> Jonson, who worked at the building of Lincoln's Inn,
> with a trowel in his hand and a book in his pocket.

Smiles's book lists and praises the innovators and inventors as well as the MPs who came from humble backgrounds, but in the following years, writing other volumes entitled *Character* (1871), *Thrift* (1875) and *Duty* (1880), his views, far from being anti-establishment, became the watchwords for middle-class opinion and government attitude to the poor. Throughout the rest of the century, emphasis was placed on the qualities of being 'upright' and 'respectable'. Part of this involved working in established trades, keeping out of public houses and attending church or chapel services. It was assumed that if one family lived correctly in a community, their way of life would spread and encourage others.

But this ideal of a temperate, improving life was a long way from the reality in which the poorest townspeople lived. It was harder to follow an 'upright' course if surrounded by the dirt and depression of slum living. Those who lived in such places were marked out for suspicion by the fledgling police service and town councils. Maps of urban areas had shading to distinguish the 'lowest' and 'semi-criminal' districts with the worst streets and tenements in black.

Campaigns to 'clean up' an area usually stemmed from private reports carried out on behalf of associations for workers and other institutions and highlighted the worst aspects of slum living. Nottingham was particularly affected by slum housing issues because of the way it had become built up. Because of Nottingham's restrictions on building, local councillors passed regulations to control the construction of new homes. Even its workhouses were overcrowded and in poor condition. In the 1840s Henry Hancock published a report into workhouse provision in the city and blamed the excessive rates of child mortality on the numbers applying for relief and the lack of facilities. He complained that there were often five to a bed and that sick patients (who often attended the workhouse as the only form of medical treatment) were housed with healthy inmates. The workhouse at Southwell in Newark, near Nottingham, now owned by the National Trust, is the earliest surviving example of an institution built to cope with poverty on a grand scale. Built to prison designs of the time in 1824, it was intended to be imposing and reflect the separation of its inmates from society. Set apart from the urban centres, would-be inmates had to walk to the gate and surrender their family members, clothing and even their identity to perform menial and often pointless labour in return for food.

Many northern and Midlands towns retained slum districts until after the Second World War, but, gradually, pressure was brought to bear on authorities to improve the general appearance and atmosphere of cities. From the 1840s Acts reduced the number of hours that could be worked, controlled child labour and demanded that controls be put in place around the use of machinery. Child workers would be made to attend school at least part-time after 1888 and, in response to outbreaks of disease, public health boards employed sanitary inspectors to oversee the implementation of basic standards.

The accepted standards of living and working that were taking shape in towns and cities threw into sharp relief the lives of anyone to whom rules and reforms did not apply. Campaigners began to cast wider the net of improvement and, in doing so, some paid much more attention to canal people.

THE CRUSADER

In the late 1800s, the prolific growth of newspapers and magazines ensured that social campaigners had a wider reach for their message. Victorian Britain could be a hard and violent place – in many ways, life on the canals was little different from that of other working-class communities. Investigative journalism was a new way to lay bare these injustices, and seek public support for change. In 1885, the journalist William Thomas Stead published a series of articles in the *Pall Mall Gazette* which exposed the shady underworld of child prostitution in London. Called the 'Maiden Tribute of Modern Babylon', it led to the amendment of the criminal law, raising the age of consent for females from 13 to 16. In another piece, Stead argued that it was the responsibility of the press to be absolutely free to expose such abuses in society and that, by such campaigns, power could be given back to the people. He referred to it as 'Government by Journalism'.

Another prolific campaigner for social change, and a man shocked by what he observed on the canals, was George Smith, whose *Our Canal Population* was published in 1875. Smith was a resident of Coalville in Leicestershire and had formerly been engaged in campaigning for the rights of children working in the potteries and brickworks of the region. It was a personal mission, as he had been a child labourer himself: he was sent to work in a brickyard at the age of seven and carried clay for up to 13 hours a day. Smith began to inquire into the lives of canal children whom he regularly encountered near his home and workplace. He saw that not much had changed:

Of the children of these 100,000 boatmen not more, probably, than 2,000 will be found to attend either day school or Sunday school. Of the boatmen themselves 2 per cent as able to read and write would be a full proportion. I do not enter at present on the condition either physically or morally of this population. Very appalling are the facts within my knowledge, and these must sooner or later come out. Neither do I just now enter on the question of wages and earnings. But even these few data must satisfy, I humbly think, that there is a loud call for legislative enquiry, legislative supervision and legislative redress. On the face of it, it seems monstrous that with the Factory and Workshop Act of 1871, passed and in activity, it should be possible to have women and children herding together and employed as in these boats, so that the Education Act should be inoperable in relation to these boatmen's children. Trusting that the whole subject of our boatmen and coasting coal boat families will secure the powerful advocacy of the press so as to command legislation, I am, Sir, your obedient, humble servant G S Smith.

(8 October 1873, Dial House, Coalville, Leicester)

Smith's letters to the newspapers became regular and more vocal in his condemnation not only that conditions were so poor for boatpeople, but that the authorities were turning a blind eye to them. By the time Smith published *Our Canal Population*, the rhetoric had become more extreme and the tone with which he highlighted perceived abuses could hardly be said to be respectful towards the subjects he claimed to care so much about. 'His purely animal life,' writes Smith at one point, 'devoid of all spiritual and almost all social influences, has produced in him a low and coarse animalism.'

Reformers marked out such different ways of life as intrinsically 'wrong' and Smith proposed a remedy, a wish list of changes and improvements that included a minimum space for sleeping in a cabin, regular cabin inspections to improve conditions and mandatory education standards for canal children. Factory commissioners felt 'boat work' was far removed from factory life, and canal children couldn't be included under existing legislation. But Smith's lobbying helped bring about change in the form of the Canal Boat Act of 1877 and the Prevention of Cruelty to Children Act, later known as the Children's Charter, of 1889. These gave authorities the power to register the inhabitants of boats and record the numbers of people living aboard and their relationships to each other, to report on sanitary conditions and school attendance by children. The Children's Charter looked at the treatment of children in work and society in general and legislated against a number of abuses, from beating and starving children to setting up insurance policies to pay out in the event of a child's death.

Earlier legislation could also be used in dealing with boatmen and their families. The Canal Police Act of 1840 had resulted from complaints from boat owners about theft of goods. It allowed canal companies to create their own police forces to be stationed around lockkeepers' cottages, along the towpaths (which were also subject to higher levels of crime)

The Franks family, shown here, owned their own boats and worked for themselves instead of a company, but life on the canal was hard. The fourth child of the boat's owner (and namesake) Benjamin tragically drowned after falling from the boat at Slough in 1926 aged 15.

and the inns which boatpeople used. Most crime along the towpath involved petty theft, poaching and trespass or fighting between boatmen and local residents, but these canal forces, like the regular police, tended to focus on boatpeople: crews leaving boats and loads alone could be charged for losses by the owner. The Nottingham Constabulary Commission reported such a theft on the Trent: of bales of silk worth £600, although such a quantity was unusual.

George Smith wanted to improve conditions for the groups he wrote about, but was specifically interested in 'normalizing' them. His writings concentrate on topics which Smith knew would arouse the most feeling and condemnation among consumers of moralistic and improving literature. *Our Canal Population* complains about women washing over the sides of narrow boats topless: having already stated, with few exceptions, most boatpeople were filthy, Smith goes on to condemn the practice of washing because it was not done privately. There was little privacy to be had aboard, water for washing was difficult to heat and there were few opportunities to use public bathhouses. The women Smith had noticed washing did so because – apart from the fact that canal water was not particularly clean – it was the safest course of action. Very few boatpeople could swim, even though many canals had shallow lengths; they were aware of the dangers involved and saw the waterways as a workplace, not a playground.

One of Smith's bugbears was people who viewed itinerants as living a 'free' and romantic lifestyle. A number of artists chose to represent this way of life as an idyllic return to nature, countering mass urbanization. The Welsh artist Augustus John, who lived with and painted Romani Gypsies at the end of the nineteenth century, was particularly popular with middle-class bohemians and aesthetes who despised modern industrialism. Smith had no patience with it:

> The dramatist has strutted the gipsy across the stage in various characters in his endeavour to change his condition.
>
> After the fine colours have been doffed, music finished, applause abased and scene ended, he has been a black, swarthy, idle, thieving, lying blackguard of a gipsy, STILL.

These words were written by Smith after his works on canals, as he changed his focus to roadway travellers. He tried to get a bill through to place measures upon these itinerants in the 1890s. It failed to be passed.

The very fact that George Smith 'moved on' from children in the brickworks to canal people then to gypsies suggests something of his motivations. He seems to have at first been stirred by a sense of injustice at perceived abuses, then, once he had a 'cause', wrote in extremely derogatory terms in order to win others. Critical thought often gave way to vented spleen and gradually the various paths of interest he chose led him further and further from his sphere of understanding and into a situation where he had become so obsessed with his causes that the financial stability of his own family was threatened when he was fired from his job as a result of agitating and absence.

In a letter to 'the Gentlemen of the Press' dated 28 February 1882, Smith described going to a boat to talk to the children in it (the oldest a ten-year-old girl) about their lives and whether or not they knew any letters:

> Just as she was in the midst of her pitiful tale her father came 'storming' along the towing-path, the sight and sound of whom sent the poor little girl into tears. With much persuasion and a little tact I turned aside the threatened vengeance, and on the poor girl sped her way at the heels of the horse, shouting with a trembling screaming voice, 'Come up'. If the Canal Boats Act of 1877 was made a living reality, in accordance with the amending bill I am humbly promoting, instead of a dead letter, as is now almost the case, through a few faulty pieces in the act of 1877, this and many thousands of cases, similar in many respects, would be impossible.

In numerous letters to the papers and to Parliament, Smith complained that the 1877 Act was unenforceable as the metropolitan districts rarely fulfilled their responsibilities, preferring to 'let sleeping dogs lie'. When they did get involved, he said, sufficient steps were not taken to prevent abuses. In the *British Medical Journal* of December 1879, the Medical Officer of Rotherhithe, Benjamin Browning, concurred. Browning reported that, a year since the Act, the duty of inspecting 492 boats was impossible and that when a case of an unsanitary boat was found, the family 'escaped' before they could be detained. He went on to say that the Act had been 'entirely a failure' and that the only way forward would be to secure amendments giving more powers to stop boats.

It is little wonder some of the people Smith was encountering refused him access and, in some cases, threatened him with violence. In fact, Smith's image of the angry father storming along the towpath might be less to do with his perception of the child's 'treachery' and more with his own interference.

> *Aye Georgie's the lad that'll show em*
> *He'll teach them their P's and Q's,*
> *When he goes down from Coalville to London*
> *They'll see a man what don't know how to lose.*

He's give of his best for the Brickies
For once he was a brickyard child himself
But now he has fought all their battles
And used up all his hard earned wealth.

He rose from a child in the brickyards
To manage a firm all on his own,
But he lost all his money and lost his job
When he fought the children's cause all alone.

Well he won an act of Parliament for the Brickies
Though he's got no job, three children and a wife
Now he's fighting for the navigation children
And living on handouts every day of his life.

You'll see him by day at the cutside
As he talks with the boatees and their wives
By night he writes his letters to the papers
To tell the world about the boatmens lives.

Now some say he's a stubborn do-gooder
Who'd do best to look unto himself
But some of us believe he's a hero
And we'll follow him in poverty and wealth.

('Good Ol' George' by Jon Raven)

INFLUENCE ON POPULAR CULTURE

It is unlikely that Smith had many boatmen fans at the time of his campaigns; there are a number of references made to him being offered 'a swim in the cut', but he did have numerous admirers in higher places. His biographer Edwin Hodder wrote in 1896 that his character was 'difficult to define', being strengthened by the adversity he had faced in life but weakened by success and praise. Despite Smith's shortcomings, Hodder found his dogged ambition to achieve his aims admirable.

Smith was anxious that children attend school and was dismayed that church services and Sunday schools were seldom attended; Sunday trading hours didn't apply on the canals as every day was a working day. The parliamentary select committee looking into Sunday trading in the 1840s had come to realize that it would be impossible to regulate this sort of work as crews were under tight deadlines and didn't have the luxury of a day moored up.

The practical nature of such a life meant that apart from highlighting illiteracy and poverty, godlessness or even child cruelty, Smith knew that one subject above all would resonate with adult readers. His reports, diaries and letters repeatedly levelled moral accusations against the people he studied. But his views made their way into fiction, too. The canal-based novels of L. T. (Elizabeth Thomasina) Meade were directly influenced by George Smith; *Water Gypsies* was one of over two hundred books she wrote for children. Although relatively unknown today, Meade's work was very popular at the time, and her books probably did most to spread Smith's message. They were usually published by church organizations and were often serialized in magazines to be read aloud to the family. The author's main point was the lack of church attendance or belief in Jesus Christ among boatpeople. In *Water Gypsies*, the character Aunt Kiz asks her niece on her deathbed (presumably while being given the last rites), 'What is Jesus?' This, in Meade's opinion, was what made canal people a 'race apart'. Ignorance in education, she believed, prevented them from reaching salvation through the Bible's teachings.

Other children's books – such as *Dick of the Paradise* by Alfred Colbeck and *Rob Rat: A Story of Barge Life* by Mark Guy Pearse – feature beaten children who are good at heart and only want to do their best and find God. They all contain the stereotypical drunkard father. In *Rob Rat*, the boatman Old Rat loses his Staffordshire bull terrier, Fly, and 'console[s] himself in his grief by two days' drunkenness and then by an outburst of savagery upon the wretched children'. It even features an introduction about George Smith's crusade, showing how strongly the message was imbued within the fictional story.

Illustrated picture books like *Old Lock Farm* by Annie Grey were also a good way to hammer the message home as it was harder to ignore images of children and animals being abused and drowned in the canal. The reinforcing of stereotypes and demonizing of this way of life meant that, even in the twentieth and twenty-first centuries, considerable numbers of people believed that there was something wrong with families living on board a narrow boat permanently.

Violence on the canal was reported by commissioners and evidence of it appeared in newspaper reports, but too infrequently to prove that people were any more at risk on the canals than elsewhere during the period. The story of Christina Collins, found dead in the canal at Rugeley near Cannock on the Trent and Mersey in the summer of 1839, rocked Victorian society. 'Murder on the Oxford Canal: The Story of Joanna Franks', a Victorian fictionalized account written some years later, eventually inspired *The Wench Is Dead*, an Inspector Morse mystery by twentieth-century crime writer Colin Dexter. The real Christina was raped and murdered by the canal boat crew with whom she was travelling to meet her boatman husband. The crew were hunted down and ultimately hanged in front of 10,000 onlookers.

Shocking as this story was, it was not necessarily representative of any larger trend on the waterways. At this time, most women and children did not live aboard, but in cottages. There were many such tales of 'outrage' reported in the Victorian press, but nearly all of them occurred in or around places of permanent habitation.

There were, though, elements of truth about some accusations made of aspects of canal life and work. One, levelled at both crews and companies, was that there was no attempt at regulating the hiring of temporary crew. This was a problem because, since a boatman was free to subcontract, he could hire labour at a price he could determine, and either make use of itinerants along the route or of young people, whose labour was arranged through their families. In a large family, it might seem to make sense to 'sell off' the labour of an older child, especially if you already had a significant number of family members to assist on your own boat. This worked a little like the indenture system of old, where a child worker could be bound over for a number of years or apprenticed to a person known to the parents. There had been complaints about the apprenticeship system in workshops and factories, and a number of abuses noted, such as failure to provide adequate food or shelter or mistreatment by masters. In the first half of the nineteenth century, campaigners such as Richard Oastler and Lord Shaftesbury had argued against the indenturing of poor children from the south of England and rural parishes, being sent to work as operatives in northern factories under the 'apprentice indenture system'.

Although legislation had stopped this by the 1870s, there were still plenty of instances of mistreatment of youth in factories, with overlookers' use of belts and straps as well as misuse of personal power often covered up during visits by inspectors. It was common for a poor family to try to hide the true age of a city child, in order to allow them to work sooner. Periods of slump and unemployment often led to falsifying of documents – or use of someone else's – to suggest a child was of age, as children on low wages would always find work. Poorly fed and housed children were small and slight, so determining age physically was often difficult. There were numerous incidents of boys going by one name at home and another at work, or being sent on 'errands' when inspectors paid their visits. Inspectors did record cases of 'uncertainty' on factory visits, but few employers faced large fines for breaking rules, and families where the main breadwinner was absent or out of work were often unable to resist the potential extra wages of children in employment.

On the canals it was a different matter. It was difficult for the authorities to determine if a child in a case of reported cruelty or accident was part of the family or not. It was easy to 'disappear' on the network; children's births were not always recorded, and baptisms, when they happened at all, could be years after the birth and happen 'all at once' at places of convenience. George Smith complained that a man and woman who were living together while unmarried were unlikely to admit this to the authorities, and were equally less likely to be candid about the ages of children or their employment. The Children's Charter gave the state more powers than ever before to intervene in family life and, if necessary, remove a child from a situation through the power of the courts, but few councils were prepared to do this, knowing that the alternative would be the workhouse or parochial school.

Some well-publicized cases around the time of *Our Canal Population* highlighted the difficulties of regulating child labour on the canals. One was the violent death of Elizabeth Lowke, aged eight, in July 1875 at Bushbury in Wolverhampton. In December of that year, a couple, Frederick and Elizabeth Musson, were tried for Elizabeth's murder at the Staffordshire Winter Assizes. Her father testified that he, as a single parent, had arranged for her to care for the couple's baby in return for food and clothing. Other witnesses (all canal employees or boatmen) stated that the couple had been seen abusing the girl with a whip and fists. The canal company clerk, Charles Millington, also testified that he had been called to the boat when the girl did not get up one morning. He found her dead, with numerous injuries, lacerations and bruises. The cause of death was determined to have been blows to the head causing internal bleeding.

In the defence presented by Mr Justice Plowden (the couple had no representative) he began by asking the jury to ignore comments made in the press about canal life and to try to forget their 'prejudices' and consider manslaughter rather than murder. On the verdict of manslaughter, the presiding judge admonished the father for neglect. He made a point of saying that, had the verdict been murder, he would have sentenced both to execution, but he had no other choice than to prescribe the strongest sentence possible: 20 years' hard labour.

Inquest records in areas served by waterways have numerous listings of deaths in and around canals. The *Liverpool Journal* of 27 January 1877 reported the case of 'Mrs Downes, wife of a joiner, suffering from melancholia for some time, who drowned her eleven year old son in the Ashton canal at Droylsden [in Greater Manchester] and then jumped in herself'. The same week the coroner recorded the death of an eight-year-old boy, badly mutilated in the canal, who had been missing since November.

Despite such publicized cases, most canal deaths proved to be accidental. Some were to do with falling and crushing injuries from boats and cargo, others caused by burns, lacerations and accidents with boilers and motors. One such example is the death by accidental drowning of three children from the same family in the Leeds and Liverpool Canal at Shipley in 1863. Thornton Kendall, aged nine, while playing near their Windhill home fell into the cut with his sisters, Olive, aged seven, and Hannah, aged four. The canal is not particularly

THE FAMILY: THE EAST MIDLANDS

deep at 4 to 7 feet, but these children would not have been able to swim, and were playing unsupervised. Although it was perfectly normal for children to be out of doors, the area where they lived was an industrial environment and people were often lured into a false sense of security of canal towpaths as safe places. The black-edged funeral card printed by the parents, George and Sarah, includes a commemorative poem with one verse reading:

> But what security is breath,
> Against the Uplifted hand of death?
> Not one is safe, not one secure.
> Not one can count a moment sure.
>
> (Collections of Bradford Museums and Galleries)

SOCIAL SHIFTS

The 1877 Canal Boat Act prescribed minimum standards for canal life, including specifying the number and the age of children sleeping on board. But it did not cover the issue of child labour, and made no effort to ensure that its provisions were enforced. For George Smith, the Act was a watered-down version of the remedies he had proposed. He did not give up, though, and continued to bombard the press with lurid tales of horrific conditions on the canals. Thanks largely to his efforts, the Act was eventually amended to ensure that inspectors would make regular checks for overcrowding and to require canal children to attend school.

By then, though, George Smith was a broken man. His years of campaigning had come at a heavy cost, mostly funded out of his own pocket. He'd lost everything – even his family home. There's no doubt that the laws he helped to implement before his death in 1895 improved the lives of thousands of children. Although his motives were religious, dogmatic and evangelical, like many Victorian reformers, he was justified in his comments about the lack of education in the community, and the low numbers attending church. Schooling could never be easy when a family was itinerant, but campaigners suggested that attending church should be easier for canal families. Missionaries on the cut realized that canal folk, if separated from the rest of society, would be unwilling to go into town or village to church where they might not be made welcome.

One way around this was to create special facilities for boatmen who wished either to learn their letters or to worship. At transport hubs such as Braunston, missionaries could put up tents or even hold 'floating services' aboard converted boats. The 'missions' were based along the principles of those established earlier for sailors. Philanthropists and preachers had found that ex-sailors were likely to be impoverished and disabled and needed more than just the word of God. In the same vein, boatmen's missions would have to offer incentives to promote faith, such as access to other services like medical care and provision of clothing, leisure and music, and in some even a free meal.

Where a floating chapel was made available, it was more likely to be used as an alternative to a pub, if money was tight. Sixty such boats and wharf-side shacks were built by various church missions, and their impact cannot be easily determined. In the towns and cities, mission halls were regularly attended by the poorest people, especially those who offered a 'cottage service' in the warm and dry or the added bonus of a magic lantern show entertainment or a talk by a guest speaker. Numbers didn't necessarily mean 'believers' in slum environments, as conditions forced most people to be 'out of doors' the majority of the time. Evenings or Sundays passed in relative warmth and comfort, especially in winter, proved a draw.

The idea of boat missions was not a new one. As early as 1820 a few preachers had ventured out in wooden skiffs to minister to men, and reports to the parliamentary select committees in the 1840s talked of the establishment of a network of such buildings. One called the Weaver Churches Bill in 1844 asked that provision might be made compulsory, although the petitioners made it clear that they did not want to accuse canal companies and employers of neglect.

On the broader canals at least, a condemned barge, *vulgo* a flat, may be converted at trifling expense into a floating chapel, suitable for a congregation of 150 adults. We can bear witness that such have been filled by zealous and grateful worshippers, many of whom had never before 'with holy bell been tolled to church' ...

We think the sternest opponents of cheap churches, the greatest sticklers for spires, chancels and rood lofts, would forego his objections in favor of these arks of refuge, if he could witness their effects.

Although a 'flat' (referring to a Mersey Flat or double-ended barge used to transport building materials and conduct repairs along the River Weaver) could hold about 80 tons of materials, it wasn't particularly practical or realistic to hold moving services on them in open water.

An example of this type of converted barge was the boatman's chapel in Oxford, which was moored up at Castle Mill Stream and consecrated by the Bishop of Oxford in 1839. It provided both a Sunday service for boatpeople and a Sunday school for their children, and had more than 100 pupils by the 1850s, by which time it was opening daily. Funded by local philanthropists, the chapel had been the idea of local coal merchant Henry Ward, but when, in 1868, Ward donated land for a permanent church at a nearby site known as Jericho, the chapel closed. Soon afterwards, as one contemporary account put it, 'Being possessed of less endurance than the Vicar, and probably weary and disgusted with its poor surroundings, it quietly sank one Sunday morning. It was not worth raising.'

A handful of such craft remain, as well as a modern UK canal boat mission: the Boater's Christian Fellowship of independent preachers and members, formed in 1995, who operate a programme of sermons and events in the mission style. Since 2004 a boatman's chapel in St Peter's Church (a converted Dutch barge) has been moored in West India Quay in London, through the ministry of St Anne's Church close to Canary Wharf. These new floating missions are designed to attract those who live on the cut or around the urban waterfronts today.

ALTHOUGH CARRYING FAMILIES hung on for longer in the East Midlands than in other regions, the competition from rail couldn't be argued with. Falling profits for both canal companies and carriers dropped to the point that lines had to amalgamate or sell to the railways. Many experiments had been made with motors and steam towing as well as engines to operate lifts and inclined planes, but it seemed that as an industry the boatman's best days were behind him. Today, canals are only responsible for around 3 per cent of haulage in the UK, and most narrow boat dwellers are not doing this work. They are not generally related to the generations of canal folk who made a living on the waterways before 1960 either. Rather, most of those who currently own or live on a boat do so as a leisure interest or for the alternative lifestyle they represent in the twenty-first century.

Father Christmas visits the narrowboat 'Natal' in 1934. By this time, British people were experiencing a more homogenized culture, exposed to cinema, radio and colour magazines. The appearance of Father Christmas is based on a mainstream culture, which canal families were still seen as separate from. The family on the boat are wearing old-fashioned clothing compared to observers along the towpath.

Life on a houseboat today continues to be seen by some as a nostalgic and idealistic existence. In the 1970s, barges could be bought and restored cheaply, offering prospective boatpeople a chance to have a home which was economical to run and didn't fit into the homogenized suburban environments on the outskirts of most cities. Neglect around remote waterways and poor levels of investment meant that moorings were affordable even for people on low wages. Communities on the fringe, artists, and 'new age' families were drawn towards a new kind of community. These people were supplemented by those who made boating a hobby or who 'retired' to barges, to live off pensions and the proceeds from selling their houses. Although there was initially some tension between the remaining working families and these new so-called 'noddy boatmen' (see page 283), it remains true that people who choose not to holiday but to make their lives permanently on the water are still widely distrusted by settled communities.

Once again, the numbers of people living permanently on barges and narrow boats is difficult to calculate, but the Canal and River Trust estimates that if a third of boat owners live on them permanently, the numbers should be around 11,000. The scale of use of popular canals across the country is evidence of a revived interest and appreciation in these networks since they ceased to be purely industrial. The growing numbers of boats, both restored and new, are keeping alive time-honoured skills which would otherwise have died out. Yards such as LMBS (Lymm Marina Boat Sales) at Warrington Lane in Cheshire are able to build boats and fitments to order as well as repair older craft.

A change in the background of these residents has led to a shift in appreciation of canals and waterfronts, steering representations towards the economies which benefit from a heritage past. The former warehouse premises of the carriers Fellows, Morton and Clayton, after being known as the Nottingham Canal Museum, is now a restaurant and bar named the Canal House. Additional visitors to locks and heritage sites create a surge in the number of tourist related income generation opportunities for the Canal and River Trust as well as an injection of money into the local services and tourism markets. Users of towpath and canal-side pubs choose these destinations because they offer on some level the chance to engage with heritage, even if in an imagined way. While the representations of easy going through fine countryside suggest a link to the pre-industrial past, the waterways and the people on them are reminders of how industry and commerce was shaped, changed and continues to develop through our own times.

6
THE DESIGNERS: BIRMINGHAM

LOOKING AT MAPS of inland waterways (see Plate 14), English canals appear to circle around Birmingham and the Midlands, spreading out from their junctions to allow boatmen to navigate in all directions, although they were not actually envisaged or built as a joined-up network. Landlocked, and miles from the coast, any trading outside the local area had to be based on rivers. Major waterways already flowed through the East and West Midlands, and by the time of increasing industrial development Birmingham was one of the first places to get an Act of Parliament passed to cut a modern canal on the back of the Bridgewater in Manchester. It was James Brindley who was called on in 1768 to build the city's oldest line, the Birmingham Canal, from Smethwick to Tipton, near Dudley in the West. After being completed, the line was improved and extended in the nineteenth century by Thomas Telford's 'New Main line', which took the terminus to Wolverhampton and beyond Smethwick to the Gas Basin at the heart of the city centre of Birmingham.

Today, Birmingham is the country's largest and most populated city after London. Even in the face of population decline in the Middle Ages, Birmingham had maintained its standing and flourished, due to its ability to prop up agricultural production with craft trades based on exploitation of locally mined metals, lime and coal. Usefully placed between the commercial south and the rapidly industrializing north, against the backdrop of a strong agrarian economy, the towns of the West Midlands formed a network of market places. Here, despite restrictions placed on trade, craftsmen came together to make the most of routes into the countryside and to other towns to sell their goods. During the sixteenth century, individual towns began to create niche markets for specialist goods, centred on small family workshops. These would grow by reputation, encouraging apprentices to travel regionally to learn particular skills. The process of turning local metal deposits into cast iron by indirect reduction was spread around iron-rich areas; but it was the development of blast furnaces in the centre of the country which was to be the basis of the growth of towns like Birmingham. Reliance on the blast furnace was only possible where there were raw materials to smelt, and nearby abundant fuel, water and timber to make charcoal. Abraham Darby's discoveries in coke smelting at Coalbrookdale in Shropshire and the development of steel working prompted investors to look for ways to use stronger and more flexible metals. The development of steam engines would not only create a demand for metals, but would in turn help to mine and process them. The soon-to-be-famous Birmingham workshops of Matthew Boulton would turn out 'what all the world desires to have ... Power'. A letter from Matthew Boulton's friend Dr James Small to James Watt in Glasgow, engaged in building a steam engine, requested: 'Get your patent and come to Birmingham, with as much time to spend as you can.' The men were to work together in order to develop engines before time ran out on their patent, and, despite the drawbacks of the workshops themselves, Birmingham was the ideal place in which to build models and fit prototypes together.

The pair also discussed work on the canals, as Watt had been engaged on a survey of the River Clyde with a view to cutting a canal. Boulton and Watt's Soho foundry north-west of Birmingham, close to Smethwick, was built in 1795 and within sight of the first Birmingham Canal.

> What Mr Boulton and I are very desirous of, is to move canal boats by this engine; so that we have made this model of a size sufficient for the purpose. We propose to operate without any condenser, because coals here are exceeding cheap, and because you can, more commodiously than we, make

experiments on condensers, having several already
by you. Above 150 boats are now employed on these
new waveless canals, so if we can succeed, the field
is not narrow.

(Dr James Small to James Watt, 20 September 1769)

Although the developments made in Soho were to have far-
reaching and long-lasting effects on the growth of factory
towns in other regions, the 'workshop' mentality and character

The Soho works belonging to Matthew Boulton and James Watt. They, along
with William Murdoch, worked on the development of the steam engine for
industrial uses, and were within sight of the Birmingham Canal.

remained. Termed the 'workshop of the world', its metal craft goods, manufactured in distinct quarters of the city, had gained a reputation worldwide by the late 1700s: from the north to the south and across the dominions, a man's watch, snuff box or plough blade was likely to have originated there. At the point of organization of these small trades to supply growing demand for affordable metalware, canals were being discussed as a means of regular bulk supply. During the surge of canal building and the urbanization of market towns, numerous travellers studied and surveyed the region. While making their reports, they also left to posterity their impressions of this part of the world. While men like the Welsh poet John Dyer ('the Bard of the Fleece') wrote of the city of Leeds and similar places, other remarks made about Birmingham and the towns of the Black Country were damning in their criticism of a landscape desolated by the digging for and working of iron and coal.

> Industry, which dignifies the artist, lifts the swain,
> And the straw cottage to a palace turns,
> Over the work preside.
> Such was the scene of hurrying Carthage,
>   when the Trojan chief
> First viewed her growing turrets. So appear
> The increasing walls of busy Manchester,
>   Sheffield and

Birmingham, whose reddening fields
Rise and enlarge their suburbs.

(John Dyer, Leeds, 1758)

The clustered, busy environment of Birmingham retained a character of individualism until the middle of the nineteenth century. It did not resemble northern textile towns, nor the South Yorkshire mining and steel districts. Birmingham was divided into areas of interest or 'quarters' responsible for making manufactured domestic and personal goods, as well as tools and engines for mass production and power. Products were diverse and the working people of the city experienced a variety of workplaces and conditions as a result. Since most of these industries were based on machine working and use of the abundant fossil fuels, the city quickly became overcrowded and dirty. The initially widespread and enthusiastic eulogizing of 'business' eventually took on a negative feel, as the term 'Black Country', referring to places sitting on coal seams, started to be applied to other industrial areas around Birmingham.

In *The Flower of Gloster*, written in 1911, Ernest Temple Thurston wrote about a canal journey taken on a boat of the same name through the middle of the country. He particularly remarked on the 'ruination' of the English countryside as he left Warwickshire and stated:

> You only have to go into the Black Country to
> know what can be done with a wonderful world
> when God delivers it into the hand of man ... the
> stream of molten metal flows through the veins and
> arteries of a great nation ... but what a price to pay,
> and what a coinage to pay it in ... those belching
> furnaces and that poisoned land must make you
> marvel as you pass it by.

Thurston was writing a romantic missive about the English countryside and the notion of roaming free on a voyage of self-discovery. After passing from Oxford through Warwickshire on the Thames and Severn and waxing lyrical about the quaint villages and simple characters he met, the tone of the book changed in its description of the Black Country and the 'charred heart' as an 'awful yet wonderful part of the world'.

By this point, the attractions of industrial progress had worn off somewhat. Depression and slump in English manufacturing and shocking reports about urban living conditions had led some artists and writers to the conclusion that industrialization and urban growth were responsible for many socio-economic problems and a changed culture in England. A fashion for 'looking back' had been growing since the 1880s in artistic movements as a reaction to the previous generations' busyness. The aesthetic movement and the establishment of the English Arts and Crafts movement grew out of a nostalgic longing for the 'good old days': the golden age which, to an extent, canals represented. By the end of the nineteenth century, canals (although still a working environment) had begun to appear almost tranquil and traditional in comparison to railways and the expansion of roads for buses, trams and motor cars. Cities like Birmingham were used as an example of the loss of a culture based on small and rural communities, be they real, or imagined.

> *At Whitsuntide, in days gone by. The Greybeard said*
> *to his gay Son,*
> *There was Whitsun fairs, ales and cakes and fun was*
> *all the day, Son.*
> *Wrestling bouts by the village green, playacting in the*
> *booths, Sir.*
> *Lasses so gay as never was seen, a merry merry time in*
> *sooth, Sir.*
> *Now village lads, they go to town to factories and*
> *shops, Oh.*
> *The lasses far too fine-off grown to wield the broom*
> *and mop, Oh.*
> *Farmers scarce can find a hand, to tend the beasts or*
> *hoe, Sir.*

To fell the trees, to plough the land, the scholar no
muscles grows, Sir.
But still for Whitsunday they come, by 'scursion train
so new, Sir.
To see the old folks, the village home, to bring the
children to, Sir.
For English lads love country air, in sunshine or in
rain, Sir.
I'm thinkin' that they soon might fare, back to the
land again, Sir.

('The Whitsun Fair' – English traditional folk song)

The criticisms of the layout of industrial Birmingham led in part to a later nineteenth-century transformation in both the way the city was run and the way it looked. Joseph Chamberlain was responsible for a plan to give Birmingham a 'facelift' and to reform its public organizations and council in order to make the city a better, cleaner and fairer place to live and work. These ideals of reform were to be mirrored in the architectural developments of the city; to create a stamp of identity and urban character which would be instantly recognizable and an emblem of civic pride. In an environment where there were fewer massive factories with the controlling influence that such employers were able to put into place, Birmingham's workforce was dependent on each other in its trades. Since many craftsmen were able to carry on skilled trades without competition from unskilled labour, they were better able to make demands on employers when it came to rates of pay, housing and expectations for improvement through a company or by setting up in business for themselves. There was an atmosphere of early combination and radicalism in Birmingham which led to support for the suffrage society to allow all adult working men the right to vote, as well as foster a following for liberal politics in the town. In an environment of increased communication between the classes and a leaning towards reform, a liberal association was formed in 1865. Joseph Chamberlain was not a member of the association, but had come to Birmingham as one of the 'village lads' and held a keen sense of political justice and a desire to reform through radical politics and improvement of the working people. Elected as an MP for St Paul's ward in 1869 and afterwards chosen to be the city's Mayor, he wished to reform the council to govern for the people by breaking down class control of services and institutions to impose the 'civic gospels' which it was believed would act as an equalizing measure.

The effects of Unitarian and liberal attitudes on local politics became evident in the middle of the century by the building of numerous chapels and institutions where people would be better able to learn and improve the city. Visitors noted that the city was crowded with homes of the working population, but that the suburban areas were also spreading around the centre in a ring, offering the middle classes a greener, leafier alternative to the city where space was at a premium. Compared to the urban districts to the north-west in Liverpool, Manchester, Bradford and Leeds, with their slum tenements and cellar dwellings, the back-to-back houses in Birmingham were generally considered of a superior quality to those found in other manufacturing towns. There was, though, a noted lack of gardens and public spaces. It was this absence of openness and greenery which troubled writers, who commented that the areas between Midlands towns were devoid of trees and greenery, and that the urban centres spread out and formed a seething mass rather than having separate identities.

> About Wolverhampton, trees, grass and every trace
> of verdure disappear. As far as the eye can reach, all
> is black, with coal mines and iron works, and from
> this gloomy desert rise countless slender pyramidal
> chimneys whose flames illuminate the earth.
>
> (Friedrich von Raumer, *England in 1835*)

An attempt to rectify the stark nature of the city was made by Chamberlain and the City Council to give the centre a new look based on the popular architecture admired by middle-class tourists to the Continent. Another tourist to industrial

England in the 1840s, Léon Faucher, had been horrified by some of the living and working conditions of northern factory workers, but had favourably compared Birmingham and its craft-based industry to the layout and culture of Paris. Joseph Chamberlain's ambition was to emulate the city of revolution still further by creating new boulevard thoroughfares through Birmingham. The layout of Corporation Street in 1878 heralded an interest in renaissance architecture, and in the building of paved walkways with grand and imposing sandstone buildings on either side, devoted to the public good. Chamberlain got at least some of his vision built, destroying slum dwellings in the meantime and encouraging the growth of the centre as a retail district.

> A town is a solemn organism through which shall flow, and in which shall be shaped, all the highest, loftiest and truest ends of man's moral nature.
>
> (George Dawson, Birmingham Baptist Minister, 1866)

Corporation Street was seen by Chamberlain and his followers as a way of using industry to create art and, by doing so, inspire working people to invest in their city and commit their talents to it for the benefit of their fellow men. The buildings erected here to the virtues of education, in libraries, galleries, theatres and Methodist halls were one aspect of the improvements. The other significant change was the civic response to physical development; in addition to the clearing of slums to be replaced by open spaces and continental architecture, significant steps were taken to deal with the treatment of sewerage, paving and lighting. Public health acts would enable the corporation to clear middens and nuisance sites as well as buy up gas companies for regulation by local government. The Birmingham Gas, Light and Coke Company and the Birmingham and Staffordshire Gas Light Company, both opened in the early 1800s, were bought out for the city. Gas lighting was one of the main areas around which clean living and health was based. Lit streets were deterrents to crime and illuminated structures were a source of civic pride. Gas would further enable efficient use of the waterways in working at night on the fast 'rat runs' of coal which were the backbone of trade on the network.

THE BIRMINGHAM CANALS

A route to Birmingham itself had been considered as a branch for the Trent and Mersey Canal in the 1770s when the men behind it were pressing for a main line canal to connect the East Midlands with the northern cities. Apart from Josiah Wedgwood, a leading figure in the movement, his friend and physician Erasmus Darwin (grandfather of Charles), who lived in the town of Lichfield, wrote about the potential improvements that would flow from bringing coal to the towns around the region. The Trent and Mersey eventually decided against the plan, and those who wanted canals to link to Birmingham's would have to make arrangements to cut their own. At a previous meeting of potential investors at the Swan Inn on 26 January 1767, after receiving Parliament's assent to go ahead, James Brindley's survey of the area had been discussed and routes for a canal from Birmingham examined.

The Birmingham Canal opened on 6 November 1769, and the town was soon overloaded with local coal. This was to be effective in making Boulton and Watt's experiments cheaper than originally expected. Mine owners and canal men alike realized that if they were going to get the best prices for their coal, and make money on tolls, the canal would need to be extended out of Birmingham to north and south.

Accusations of monopoly on the original Birmingham Canal led to discussion of a line through from coal-rich Walsall to Lichfield, via Fazeley, to form a junction with the Coventry Canal. Plans to extend this route right through to Birmingham represented a threat of competition from further north, and the Birmingham Company was concerned, 'It appearing to this company not only unnecessary, that any other canal be made to this town, but that the same if made would greatly prejudice the present undertaking.'

The company was right to be worried. Its former chairman, Samuel Gabbett, had resigned over his original backing of the plans for the Trent and Mersey extension. The new company had permission and enough subscriptions to go ahead, and this forced the Birmingham Canal Company to consider amalgamating the two canals under one organization: the Birmingham Canal Navigation. This early union, in 1784, would be the pattern for how the Midlands canals were to operate in the future, and would be partly responsible for the numerous branches and cuts spiralling out from the centre of Birmingham. Many of the companies arranged deals and mergers with each other, so that the region itself held a monopoly on goods traded. By 1825, Birmingham Canal Navigation owned 70 miles of canal around the town, and therefore had a larger operating waterway network than the Italian city state of Venice.

Birmingham and Fazeley were amalgamated in 1784 with the Birmingham Company and built from Farmer's Bridge, initially under the leadership of John Smeaton. This was to be an unusual set of locks and tunnels constructed underneath the expanding city, dropping down from the Gas Basin, and requiring lighting in the subterranean darkness. Today, the urban section of the canal dips underneath the hub of roadway known as Spaghetti Junction; this is the modern equivalent of the web of canals clustered around the city, subject to equally heavy traffic on its way to all parts of the UK. Pressure at this point and throughout the Midlands network by the 1820s required not only the locks to be kept open at night, but also improvements and short cuts to be made under the advice of Thomas Telford in order to speed up the journeys with the threat of rail now on the horizon.

> There are nearly 70 steam engines, and about 124 wharfs and works already seated on the banks of the canal, between Farmer's Bridge and Aston.
>
> (1839 report case in support of the Birmingham canal bill, BPL 177408)

As part of improvements to the Birmingham Canal, a reservoir at Rotton Park was recommended, as was an aqueduct at Smethwick to allow the old Birmingham line to pass over the new one, cut through the summit. Works were begun along the amalgamated line to relieve pressure in what was by now a heavily built-up area.

After the passing of a bill in 1791 for a southerly route to be built, an agreement was made between the Worcester and Birmingham and Dudley canals to form an extension route for the coal of Dudley to reach the River Severn, Oxford and

London. This direct competition resulted in an injunction being taken out against the company by Birmingham Canal Navigation, preventing the line coming into contact with their own property. This was enforced by the erection of the 'Worcester bar', a physical barrier placed on the basin of the Worcester and Birmingham, so that any goods being taken from one line to the other had to be unloaded and loaded again over the bar between boats. Repeated attempts were made to resolve the dispute and remove the hugely inconvenient bar. It was eventually lifted in 1815 with a 'communication lock'; the drawback was that tolls were now charged, supposedly for the reasons of water conservation and maintenance. These tolls were to remain in place throughout the commercial life of the waterways as the rivalry between the two companies continued.

Among the features of the looped lines are the aqueduct and bridges designed by Thomas Telford. These were constructed in iron rather than stone, partly because of local supply and expertise in construction from casting, but also because Telford preferred to build metal bridges as the tensioning through the ironwork placed less pressure on the abutments in arched bridges. Using iron also meant being able to display decorative features in lattice patterns and complex openwork, and to experiment with colour.

DESIGN ON CANALS

From vast factory sites to the wonders of transport engineering in the form of bridges, aqueducts and lifts, eighteenth- and nineteenth-century industrial designs always made an enormous impression on visitors, writers and artists. Although they would be both romanticized and denigrated in later years, the changes driven by industry were initially attractive as well as astounding for most middle-class people. Young people visiting towns and cities made a point of travelling to see industrial concerns, and reported their findings to friends and family. Entrepreneurial characters were quick to take advantage of this fashion for progress by operating transport services to sites lying outside of the urban centres, as well as opening up hotels and inns.

Canals were now a source of interest in themselves, and the structures that appeared alongside them were equally fascinating for locals and for tourists. The Bridgewater was the first to experience a demand for 'packet boats' to tour the route between the coal mines and urban Manchester, but it was the aqueduct which proved the biggest draw. There was a gradual acceptance of the notion of using canals as a network of transportation and of communication. The immediate effects of this were first seen in the crossing of four canals around Birmingham in 1790, with specialist products from the Midlands and mid-Wales now being easily moved around the country. Cheaper carriage of building materials alone directly resulted in a physical change in the landscape. Where there was an important stopping place or loading area for goods, an economy could be based upon canal services. Repair yards and shops, workshops and company offices were built with hoists and stables alongside. At trading centres, new docks were built, and their decorative features became a part of the commission from the start, rather than an attempt to beautify something functional later. Styles and designs along the canal lines now catered to individual backers' tastes, while also proclaiming the prowess of a chief engineer wishing to make a name for himself.

Although canals were not designed to be attractive to the eye, impressive architectural achievements did foster a sense of 'art overcoming nature'. Canal routes were not leafy and green, as they are today; they were stark man-made corridors cutting through fields and rolling hills. Critics and sceptics of canal schemes in the late 1700s would probably be amazed to compare the now relatively overgrown and rural ambience of many routes to the view from their windows at the time of construction. With space needed for industrial buildings as well as stabling and accommodation along a cut, plant life could not be allowed to flourish. The route of one of the busy lines would have appeared neither tranquil nor green, and would not have smelt particularly good. Dirty water, smoke, refuse and large amounts of human and animal waste are now largely absent from canal towpaths.

Since canal routes (even those which were later amalgamated under one company or name) were cut at different times and sometimes in direct competition, there is little uniformity in standout architectural features. Some buildings, particularly bridges and canal offices or accommodation, mirror the decorative fashions of a particular period, or the taste of the architect. The shape and quality of locks varied, as did materials used, but the simple and effective design of the lock as a mechanism would be more or less the only feature which would be constant throughout the country. By locks, especially on a long or complex flight, canal companies constructed buildings according to their needs. Lock and toll keepers as well as watchmen needed a home on the cut in order to discharge their duties, and often these buildings needed to offer additional functions such as a secure place to keep toll money or records and even, occasionally, contain a 'lockup' to keep a trespasser or thief until he could be dealt with by the authorities.

Canal-side houses varied from the simple lockkeeper's cottage – constructed from cheap local materials, usually with a space allocated to grow vegetables and perhaps keep some livestock – to elegant properties with porticos and multiple windows. Although designed as safe and secure houses, sometimes with a variety of vantage points from multi-levelled façades and windows looking in every direction, tollhouses had a more uniform appearance. The design of buildings at important points on the network with multi-angled walls was an important functional design feature. Unusually for homes at the time, most of the accommodation built alongside the towpath made good use of windows. At the time the canals were built there was no official police force beyond the watchman or private officer employed by the canal company, a toll keeper or clerk might need to be able to view the canal and approaching boats from a number of vantage points. Other examples of hexagonal, octagonal and circular tollhouses for both canals and turnpike roads are evident in parts of the Midlands, as well as in Wales, notably along the Holyhead toll road.

The toll keeper was an important figure along the cut and, having to deal with money and records, was usually a literate individual who could read letters and newspapers to crews, post notices and deal with the local authorities or neighbours on behalf of the company. The threat of theft from and violence against the 'company man' was very real; the canal could be a dark and dangerous place at night, and numerous tollhouses were attacked or suffered attempted break-ins. Some criminals employed 'distraction techniques' by calling on the tollhouse residents to assist with a perceived accident or injury, which was more likely at major junctions or while navigating through lock systems. The double-fronted junction house at King's Norton on the Birmingham and Worcester Canal, built in 1796, is typical of the style and practicality of the canal companies, displaying their toll prices and enforcing them in an outwardly reserved and respectable manner (see Plate 15).

Tollhouses were generally small. The brick 'castle' constructions of rounded tollhouses on the Birmingham and Fazeley Canal mirrored the simpler structures found on the Staffordshire and Worcester. The popular decorative style named 'roses and castles' on boats features painted representations of fortified structures and towers, set in a background of natural flowers and plants. Although the origins of the painting style on boats themselves is obscure, the murals reflect a number of examples of architecture associated with the English countryside and tales of days gone by. The tradition of symbolic painting seems to stem from the widespread change to lifestyles based around the family and itinerant community.

Once the period of regular toll collecting and monitoring ended, some tollhouses fell into disrepair or were demolished. Surviving examples are preserved by the Canal and River Trust, and are often used as visitor centres and display spaces. Perhaps appropriately, one Walsall turnpike road tollhouse was adapted to serve as a pub and restaurant – the other common remaining feature of the waterways to survive is the towpath alehouse. The pubs left along the busiest routes in the country survive today mainly because of an upsurge in the fortunes of the canals as leisure hot spots. Although popular on summer evenings in modern times, canal-side inns were an essential part of the maintenance of the canal itself in the early rush to build in the late eighteenth century and remained vital to Victorian carrying trade. When a canal was being dug, the local alehouses accommodated surveyors, engineers and other visiting parties. They were places where business deals could be made and committee meetings held. They offered somewhere to buy hot food, send for ordered goods, hear the news and hire new hands. Boatmen with no fixed address, and without easy access to towns or villages, had to rely on the landlords of pubs for local news, or to leave messages for other passing families on the coal runs through the Midlands. Pubs close to the towpath were lifelines for communication as everyone would pass them sooner or later.

Most pubs lining the waterway are old buildings and some of them date in unaltered form from the construction of the canals themselves, and still bear names like the Navigator and the Old Boatman. Some remaining watering holes predate the canals and give a sense of what life might have been like in rural parts before the Industrial Revolution. The Jolly Sailor at Saltford, overlooking a lock on the River Avon – part of the Kennet and Avon Canal – was built before the canal in 1726 and a painted panel in the bar shows the canal at the time of its construction. On the Birmingham and Fazeley, the White Horse at Sutton Coldfield was later joined by establishments like the James Brindley in the Gas Basin.

The proliferation of drinking establishments helped foster the reputation of navvies and canal boatmen for hard drinking and trouble after hours. Some newspaper reports of trouble around alehouses mention the requirement of reading the 'riot act' to crowds who had become aggressive and started spoiling for a fight after one too many. Pubs gained reputations for attracting drunkards, but in practice this was rarely the case; boatmen were on tight turnaround schedules and needed to be able to continue their journeys after mooring up. Pubs provided a vital service and some could be built in grand style to attract the custom of the canal and carrying companies as well as the ordinary workers. Those houses which remained in business into the nineteenth century were forced to adapt by becoming hotels or offering service to passing road traffic, which involved building roadways at the backs of their buildings to maintain trade. Today, though, the original purpose of those buildings remains clear. Looking at these inns today, their shape and size, projection towards or offset from the water and design gives away their primary function, be it navvy alehouse, boatman's retreat or modern leisure development.

BUILDING IN THE MODERN AGE

> I found adjacent to this great and flourishing town, a canal of little better than a crooked ditch, with scarcely the appearance of a hailing path, the horse frequently sliding and staggering in the water, the hailing line sweeping the gravel into the canal, and the tangling of boats incessant; while at the locks at each end of the short summit, crowds of boatmen were always quarrelling or offering premiums for a preference of passage, and the mine owners, injured by the delay, were loud in their just complaints.

(Thomas Telford on visiting Birmingham in 1825)

Thomas Telford's approach to design was to concentrate on the practicalities and ease of use of the road, canal or dock he might be planning. St Katharine Docks in London, for example, was clearly not designed with aesthetics in mind.

Telford planned the dock next to the Tower of London after completion of work on the Menai Bridge, which spanned the

strait to Anglesey in North Wales. The area for the dock had
to be cleared of very heavily populated housing, and the site
was limited in size and had to take into account the ebb and
flow of the Thames. The way the river followed its course, and
the need for a deep dock, meant that it couldn't be designed in
a rectangular shape. Separated into east and west docks from
the entrance basin and designed to be pumped out as needed
for repairs and cleansing, water would flow in again quickly
no matter if the tide was high or low. The whole outline of
the dock was lined with ample warehousing, workshops and

St Katharine Docks had been open since 1828, designed by Thomas Telford to
make the best possible use of limited space with two basins and warehouses built
to be directly loaded from boats. The pumping engines to maintain the water
levels from the Thames were supplied by Boulton and Watt's manufactory.

offices via large pillared warehouse doors under permanent cover to protect goods while unloading.

Where decoration or break from architectural norms becomes apparent, it is clear that the influence of an individual has been brought to bear. This might be the family crest or the symbol of a wealthy patron, or even of someone whose land has been cut through, marking the significance of the action for those passing and reminding them whose land they are permitted to pass through.

In some cases, particularly in designs for features such as bridges, engineers saw the construction as an opportunity to put more into the style of their work, in order that the feat of engineering was appreciated as a benefit and not considered a blot on the landscape.

The Birmingham and Fazeley Canal displayed a number of features of pure functionality fitting the layout of the city at the time of building. Using large quantities of red and black brick for lining and bridges, a large section of the route leading out of the city was cut low and walled in, so the line appeared dark and subterranean in places. This led to its nickname: Bottom Road. The use of brick is also apparent in the tollhouse cottage at the junction with the Coventry at the towpath bridge. Short, squat, rounded bridges with simple, economical arches are designed with the needs of a towing horse in mind, with ridged brick-laid paths and cut through to assist towing around corners and on to other lines. These early bridges feature steep, humpbacked arches in stone, or in areas like the Midlands and Staffordshire, where there were plenty of them, bricks. One bridge along the Birmingham and Fazeley route provides a useful emergency feature in its small arched chamber set into the brickwork. Called a 'stop plank store', poles could be left here to be used in cases of a breach of the canal banks, in order to stop the towpath from slipping into the cut, which would both stop traffic and cause a terrible blockage.

Often, where lack of space stops a towpath continuing, or where a boat needs to take a turn and join another water-way at a junction, a 'roving bridge' – sometimes called a 'turnover' – allows a horse to cross from one side of a canal to the other without being unhitched. Birmingham has a number of examples of this feature. The basic arched design, whether single or multi-span, had been in use for centuries and – provided it was correctly built with properly positioned abutments at each end – was economical to repair and easy to use with horses. Some of the wider examples of low bridges crossing rivers even had houses and shops built along them, such as at Pulteney Bridge in Bath.

The use of iron in the building of bridges originated in Coalbrookdale at the site of the Derby blast furnace, now a part of the heritage complex of Ironbridge Gorge. The bridge begun in 1779 was of a semi-circular, ribbed design, each section weighing over five tons and running to 80 feet in length. The pieces fitted together with mortises and dovetail joints fastened with a key, and the abutments were fixed into the riverbanks over the Severn with iron pillars set into stone. During construction, commentators were concerned that the man-made material might not be strong enough, and that the fast-flowing water would undermine the ends of the bridge, causing its collapse. Two hundred years on, the bridge is still standing but the banks have been affected by reduction and, as a result, it was decided not to allow traffic over the bridge, excepting visitors on foot.

Once proof of the properties for using cast iron had been given, the popularity of it as a material in architecture soared. Cast iron allowed bridges to be built in different styles and shapes and at advanced height, and enabled decorative features to be incorporated at no extra cost. Iron was flexible and could be used to strengthen as well as beautify essential structures. Leaving the Gas Basin in Birmingham centre on the Birmingham and Worcester Canal, for example, boats are taken over the Holliday Street aqueduct, rising over the road and a combination of brickwork with decorative iron lattice and pillars adding strength under the shallow arches.

The decorative footbridge over the cut on the Birmingham and Fazeley at Drayton Bassett is reminiscent of a Gothic style. The 'folly' footbridge was constructed on the estate of Sir Robert Peel, first Baronet of Drayton in Staffordshire and Bury in Lancashire. Sir Robert had made his fortune as a textile baron, out of his mill at Burrs in Bury, which was situated on the Manchester, Bolton and Bury Canal. He was a supporter of the canals which had helped him make his money and title, but held influence over the appearance of one on the manor land which he and his family quickly moved to after ennoblement. His son, Sir Robert, the second Baronet, was known for the setting up of the early police force, named 'Peelers' or 'Bobbies', but also for his efforts to repeal the corn laws and provide government-sponsored relief during the devastating Irish potato famines of the 1840s. Today, although the family seat at Drayton has been demolished and replaced by a theme park, a memorial tower stands overlooking the family's former home in Ramsbottom on Holcombe Hill. It was built by public subscription at the same time as a statue in the market place, with the figures of commerce and navigation supporting the figure of the politician. The Peel family motto was 'Industria', and indicates that, despite moving to the Midlands to live as a country gentleman, Robert Peel and his son both expressed an affinity with the labours of the working man. The plain and simple (some say unimaginative) stone tower at Holcombe represents the humble beginnings of the family and the

The continued use of the canal network in the West Midlands has ensured the survival of a number of traditional pieces of canal architecture, as well as unusual examples. The Drayton Bassett folly footbridge marks the crossing of the Peel family's holdings and stamps the mark of their personal taste on the Birmingham and Fazeley Canal.

difference between the perceived ostentation of the landed classes and the functional simplicity of industrial men.

The decorative tower bridge at Drayton is at odds with this simple style, having no architectural function other than to 'beautify' the stretch of canal in the area, to the resident's taste. The remaining bridge gives an insight into Sir Robert's tastes and his need to place his stamp on his new home. The style of the reinvented 'throwback medieval' look was not universally recognized as 'good taste' and, in some circles, the architectural and decorative choices of those who had made their way 'in trade' was ridiculed by more established families. Gradually, however, old landed families would find that for all their apparent lack of taste it would be the nouveau riche to whom they would turn for friendships and marriage in the coming years, in an environment of acceptance of 'new money' and ways of making it.

By comparison, in the 1770–80s, features on the canals would mostly be simple and built from locally available materials; it was unusual to use large amounts of budget money to elaborate them in a climate of pressure and over-spending. But by the close of the eighteenth century it was well established that canals would be a source of economic revenue and a form of transportation all over the country. Plans for engineering solutions started to show a greater interest in flair and style for its own sake. A designer could make a name for himself and get offers of work elsewhere if his bridge or tunnel was impressive or represented a 'first'. While Thomas Telford was most interested in solving problems, men like John Rennie were proud of their achievements and wanted to use them in part to beautify the landscape as well as adhere to the tastes of the members of the landed gentry who had a hand in their installation. This might mean including a fashionable Grecian balustrade or supporting pillars, in line with the fashions for public and cultural buildings. Part of the need to place decorative features on these constructions came from the rural location of many of the buildings and works. Sited in open country, it was felt by many designers that the industrial nature of the use of the waterways should not impinge on the feel of the land. This was especially true for border zones between authorities, where civic or company pride could be displayed and promote a feeling of confidence and permanence in the viewer.

> An architect should live as little in cities as a painter. Send him to our hills, and let him study there what nature understands by a buttress, and what by a dome.
>
> (John Ruskin, *The Stones of Venice*, 1851)

By the time Ruskin was writing, the radical urbanization that followed canal building had led to the development of factory-based economies and the railway network. This prompted some of the decorative elements of industrial architectural design to move on to grand and imposing railway stations, large public hotels to replace the coaching inns or rooming houses and civic halls side by side with commercial office blocks and department stores. Victorian writers objected to industrial sprawl taking over the 'village home' and 'green and pleasant England'.

> The straggling cottages by the road side, the dingy hue of every object visible, the murky atmosphere, the paths of cinders and brick dust, the deep red glow of the furnace fires in the distance, the volumes of dense smoke issuing heavily forth from high toppling chimneys, blackening and obscuring everything around; the glare of distant lights, the ponderous waggons which toiled the road, laden with clashing rods of iron, or piled with heavy goods – all betokened their rapid approach to the great working town of Birmingham.
>
> (Charles Dickens, *The Pickwick Papers*, 1837)

Some contemporary art work imagines Birmingham as a kind of Hades, with the blast furnaces of the West Midlands portrayed as a modern version of the gates of Hell. The 1843 report of the Midland Mining Commissioner, Thomas Tancred, agreed. Tancred complained that the city was interspersed with a network of canals at different levels, and that the whole of the city resembled a 'vast rabbit warren' with underground levels filled with workshops and joined to the rest of the Black Country by scarred landscapes.

Towards the end of the nineteenth century, however, water-ways began to be associated with leisure. Magazine journalism started to cover the dos and don'ts of going on the water. In 1893, the journalist Charlotte Elizabeth Humphry, writing as 'Madge' in the magazine *Truth* for a column called 'The Girl's Gossip', gave her readers advice on social customs, writing invitations and housekeeping as well as guidance about taking up any fashionable practices such as bicycle riding. Madge's advice for boating suggests that the ideal costume should follow the look and feel of that worn for the seaside but in a less precisely tailored form, and that while 'an amount of ornamentation is allowable, lace trimmed white petticoats and black patent shoes are equally out of place for both, suiting not the nature of a boat'.

Within 60 years, any industrial and carriage use for canals had all but ceased. The remaining cuts in regular use were dominated by leisure boatmen (see Plate 2). Some of the old lockkeepers and carrying men referred to these as 'noddy boatmen',* who had no place to get to and failed to understand the way boats and cuts operated. The 1920s also brought an increase in the use of faster motorboats, which caused churning and backwash along the canal sides, silting up tunnels and eroding banks. There were numerous incidents

---

* Midlands slang for a stupid or incompetent person.

involving stuck craft, broken or blocked locks, and neglecting to close locks properly. Criticism and rivalry between the old and new residents of the water grew.

The transformation and restoration of disused waterways was made possible by the upswing in the use of canals, their towpaths and wealth of architecture and industrial heritage as a focus for the leisure and tourism market. Birmingham's Gas Basin today is the site of modern shops, bars and restaurants in a complex called the Mailbox, a former Royal Mail site. The area is characterized by modern design and architecture including a building known as the Cube, close to Birmingham University buildings. Here, a leisure economy based on industrial heritage and proximity to a waterside is complemented by contemporary architecture aimed at younger, city-dwelling residents. As elsewhere in the country, the former goods warehouses that line the canal and basin are desirable properties for redevelopers, thanks to their size and the unique features they offer. As development space is at a premium for most overcrowded British cities, property companies have found that buying cheap disused inner-city industrial sites has allowed them to capitalize on increasing interest in regenerated environments. The Birmingham and Fazeley Canal to the north also incorporates modern design elements among the toll offices and cottages of the Georgian Cambrian Wharf by Farmer's Bridge. Here, the dark tunnels of Bottom Road have been opened to turn the subterranean urban wasteland into a route through the centre. Brick-built walkways have been constructed to preserve a heritage feature while providing additional facilities in a highly populated and built-up area.

Travelling on Birmingham's canals allows an architectural journey into the past. On the Birmingham and Worcester, the route south takes travellers past a number of landmarks designed before and after the building of this stretch of water, by which to compare construction methods as well as design. A comparison of the medieval Worcester cathedral at the end of the line to the Severn with the modern industrial developments along the line is eye-opening. The cathedral, continuing as a secular chapter of canons after the dissolution of the monasteries, has the only circular chapter house of the early English cathedrals and perhaps suffered less under the reformation of Henry VIII as the elaborate fan-vaulted roof and delicate stone tracery was erected to the memory of his elder brother Prince Arthur. Built over Norman stonework, the rib and panel ceiling is a marvel of architectural engineering in its own right and, viewed from the river, rises impressively to stand out in the local landscape.

On the outskirts of Birmingham, the Bournville site was also designed, by use of the waterway, to stand out from the crowd. The Cadbury brothers, George and Richard, had managed their cocoa production firm from the centre of Birmingham but relocated south-west along the canal, into what was a rural environment, where plans for a model community were made and drawn up by the architect W. A. Harvey. This industrial village would be unlike most others: it could be lived in by working-class people who did not have to work at Cadbury's plant, as long as they complied with the rules of the village trust. The site was chosen because of its distance from Birmingham and its access to green fields, trees and water. Although the canal side was a place of work and industry, the design was made to feel rustic and comparable to the 'village home' that a resident's grandparents might have left behind for city work. Facilities for the residents were designed around a 'village green', and Harvey even went to the extent of reconstructing old buildings on the site to give it an air of rural authenticity. The streets were named after trees, flowers and other natural forms and the site now had what commentators earlier in the nineteenth century had noticed was missing in Birmingham: green space. The idea of the model village was well known in industrial hubs, and another chocolate manufacturer, Joseph Rowntree, established a similar village on the edge of York.

At the time of its construction, Bournville was a superior alternative to overcrowded Birmingham, and its aesthetic ideal was to lead by example and create an affordable blueprint

The model community of Bournville, built on the outskirts of Birmingham
around the Cadbury's chocolate factory, was a relatively late addition to
the concept of the model community. It was unique in its recreation
of a rural village atmosphere for healthy living and leisure.

for working-class life in the future as a direct reaction to
the urbanization of the industrial boom years. It is hardly
surprising that some of the support for such initiatives and
enthusiasm for building 'out' came from a backlash against
the very nature of the Industrial Revolution and the nature of
the architecture it had produced in urban areas. The artist and
designer William Morris was a supporter of such schemes and
wrote about the dejection felt by manual operatives who could
not be proud of their homes or feel free to express themselves.

He argued that a workforce living in clean, quiet and happy homes would not just be more productive, but in turn would beautify their places of work. In this way, he believed, rather than cities constantly spreading outwards, country retreats should encroach on towns and bring light where it was dark.

The architectural historian Walter Godfrey, writing in the 1940s, bemoaned a lack of interest in the concept of building with the consideration of style. He argued that 'modern' building was done with only facility and convenience in mind, and that similarity or standardization would lead to a type of pattern building so that all cities would end up 'looking the same'.

> Let us approach architecture with the firm conviction that beauty is the only excuse for its existence. Let us realise that if it is well planned, well built and functions without fault, it should please us however simple and modest may be its treatment.

Godfrey wrote these words in 1946 in a book entitled *Our Building Inheritance: Are We to Use It or Lose It?*. He and a number of eminent architects were campaigning for the restoration of historic buildings, but it would be the late twentieth and early twenty-first centuries that would see the spread of projects to restore canals and their features for a newly appreciative audience.

Today, canals are ribbons of calm, with their meandering pace and verdant borders. They are, though, as busy as they ever were – if not busier along the most popular routes at peak season – though of course, they're a long way removed from the industrial places known to the navvies and boatpeople. In the eighteenth and nineteenth centuries, living on canals was a curious way of life, and not always a desirable one. Few aspired to live on a canal – those who did so were born into this way of life or chose it out of necessity. But nowadays, canal boats are viewed as desirable residences and an alternative lifestyle choice.

The surge in the popularity of houseboats and pleasure boats has created problems for Britain's waterways – there's simply not enough space for all the boats, particularly at 'pressure points' where everyone wants a mooring. Given their popularity, are the canals becoming a victim of their own success? They were a stimulus and a catalyst to the Industrial Revolution that we've successfully converted for modern life, but some people argue that permanent mooring up was not what narrow boats were designed for, and only small numbers live a truly itinerant lifestyle. Thankfully, huge numbers of volunteers are working and fundraising to continue the development of our canals. Meanwhile, the UK's tourist boards are constantly finding new ways to attract visitors to their canals. In Scotland, for example, the Helix Complex in Falkirk offers a developed extension to the Forth and Clyde Canal between Falkirk and Grangemouth. Visitors to this ecopark can take part in a range of outdoor activities based on and around the water as well as admire the Kelpies – horses' head sculptures some 30 metres high. These dramatic pieces were modelled on a traditional working breed, the Clydesdale, and represent the Scottish spirit of inland waterways, which folklore has described as taking the shape of a horse rising from the surface.

The future of canals looks bright. People often talk about the golden age of canals, and they are usually referring to the 1800s. There's a case for saying that this, the present age, is the golden age of canals: they are in better condition (at least to modern sensibilities) than ever before, they are accessible to everybody, and many people want to use them, to travel on them, to live on them and beside them. That is the legacy of those who designed them, toiled on them and even died building them.

FURTHER READING

Jospeh Boughey and Charles Hadfield, *British Canals: The Standard History* (The History Press, 2008)

Asa Briggs, *A Social History of England* (Weidenfeld and Nicolson, 1994)

Asa Briggs, *Victorian Cities* (Penguin, 1990)

Anthony Burton, *History's Most Dangerous Jobs: Navvies* (The History Press, 2012)

Mike Clarke, *The Leeds & Liverpool Canal: A History and Guide* (Carnegie Press, 1994)

Kenneth R. Clew, *The Kennet & Avon Canal* (David & Charles, 1985)

Collins / Nicholson Waterways Guides (Nicholson, 2014)

Ultan Cowley, *The Men Who Built Britain: A History of Irish Labour in British Construction* (Merlin Publishing, 2006)

Henry Randolph De Salis, *Bradshaw's Canals and Navigable Rivers of England and Wales: A Handbook of Inland*

Navigation for Manufacturers, Merchants, Traders, and Others (Henry Blacklock and Co., 1918)

Martyn Denney, *London's Waterways* (HarperCollins, 1977)

Gary Firth, *The Leeds and Liverpool Canal in Yorkshire* (The History Press, 1999)

Stuart Fisher, *Canals of Britain: A Comprehensive Guide* (Adlard Coles, 2012)

Banister Fletcher and R.A. Cordingley, *A History of Architecture: On the Comparative Method* (The Athlone Press, 1961)

Wendy Freer, *Women and Children of the Cut* (Railway and Canal Historical Society, 1995)

David D. Gladwin, *The Canals of Britain* (Breedon Books, 1994)

Charles Hadfield, *British Canals: An Illustrated History* (David & Charles, 1984)

Charles Hadfield and Gordon Biddle, *The Canals of the British Isles* (David & Charles, 1970)

Michael Jackson and Jon Raven, *Canal Songs and Songs from Canal Folk: A Musical Documentary of the Canals* (Broadside Records, 1974)

Christopher Lewis, *The Canal Pioneers: Brindley's School of Engineers* (The History Press, 2011)

Ian Mortimer, *Centuries of Change: Which Century Saw the Most Change?* (Vintage, 2015)

David Owen, *Canals to Manchester* (Manchester University Press, 1987)

Derek Pratt, *Waterways Past and Present: A Unique Portrait of Britain's Waterways Heritage* (Adlard Coles, 2015)

Frances Pratt, *Canal Architecture in Britain: An Introduction to the Fascinating Buildings and Structures of Our Waterways* (British Waterways Board, 1976)

L.T.C. Rolt, *Narrow Boat* (The History Press, 2014)

L.T.C. Rolt, *Navigable Waterways* (Penguin, 1985)

L.T.C. Rolt, *Thomas Telford* (The History Press, 2007)

L.T.C. Rolt, *Victorian Engineering* (The History Press, 2010)

Sonia Rolt, *A Canal People: The Photographs of Robert Longden* (The History Press, 2009)

Ray Shill, *Northern Canals Through Time: Lancaster, Ulverston, Carlisle and the Pennine Waterways* (Amberley Publishing, 2014)

George Smith, *Our Canal Population* (1875; republished EP Publishing, 1974)

Malcolm I. Thomis, *The Town Labourer and the Industrial Revolution* (B.T. Batsford, 1974)

Arnold J. Toynbee and T.S. Ashton, *Toynbee's Industrial Revolution* (David & Charles, 1969)

Barrie Trinder, *The Making of the Industrial Landscape* (Orion, 1997)

Jerry White, *London in the 18th Century: A Great and Monstrous Thing* (Vintage, 2013)

Sue Wilkes, *Tracing Your Canal Ancestors: A Guide for Family Historians* (Pen & Sword Books, 2011)

Cyril J. Wood, *Manchester's Ship Canal: The Big Ditch* (The History Press, 2005)

ACKNOWLEDGEMENTS

Thanks are due firstly to Tony Parker, who approached me about doing the series and writing this book, in such a way as not to put me off entirely. To the regional producers, camera teams and research crew working on the series, for their kindness and patience with me as a novice to the world of the television presenter.

Thank you to Albert DePetrillo from BBC Books and Steve Tribe for helping me with the text under a very short deadline, and for cutting me down into manageable chunks! Thank you to all the BBC staff and freelancers who advised and ferried me from pillar to post.

My sincere thanks to the various contributors to the programme and the unseen staff and volunteers who proved so helpful to us while we were on the road, and to whom I am grateful for interesting chats about the places and buildings included.

ACKNOWLEDGEMENTS

A huge thank you to my colleagues working for Bradford Museums and Galleries, who have encouraged me to work on this project and helped to cover my workload during a very busy shoot period.

Finally, my most sincere and grateful thanks go to my parents, Mary and Terence, for their help and support and ultimately to my wonderful wife, Louise, and our children Alexander and Reah, who have been extremely patient with me working at night and away from home, and of whom I am immensely proud.

PICTURE CREDITS

BBC Books would like to thank the following individuals and organisations for providing photographs and for permission to reproduce copyright material. While every effort has been made to trace and acknowledge copyright holders, we would like to apologise should there be any errors or omissions.

16 Getty Images/Yale Center for British Art, Paul Mellon Collection, USA
24 Getty Images/Guildhall Library & Art Gallery/Heritage Images
52 Getty Images/Science & Society Picture Library
69 Alamy/©SOTK2011
72 Mary Evans Picture Library/Tom Morgan
83 Getty Images/The Print Collector
89 Getty Images/The Print Collector
99 Getty Images/Hulton Archive
117 Getty Images/Hulton Archive
133 John Billingsley / Wikicommons
135 Getty Images/Universal History Archive

PICTURE CREDITS

148 Alamy/©Chronicle
163 Topfoto/HIP
173 Getty Images/Science & Society Picture Library
183 Alamy/©Mary Evans Picture Library
196 Getty Images/Universal History Archive/UIG
215 Getty Images/Three Lions
219 Getty Images/Hulton Archive
226 Getty Images/Popperfoto
244 Getty Images/Photo by David Savill/Topical Press Agency
252 Getty Images/Science & Society Picture Library
274 Getty Images/The Print Collector
279 Alamy/©Chris Gibson
287 Getty Images/Topical Press Agency

Plate section
 1 Getty Images/Guildhall Library & Art Gallery/Heritage Images
 2 Getty Images/Universal History Archive/UIG
 3 Getty Images/Ann Ronan Pictures/Print Collector
 4 Getty Images/Science & Society Picture Library
 5 Alamy/©William Robinson
 6 Getty Images/Oxford Science Archive/Print Collector
 7 Getty Images/DEA PICTURE LIBRARY
 8 Getty Images/James Osmond
 9 Getty Images/Fine Art Images/Heritage Images
10 Alamy/©Chronicle
11 Getty Images/Hulton Archive
12 Getty Images/DEA PICTURE LIBRARY
13 Getty Images/Popperfoto
14 Mary Evans Picture Library/Mapseeker Publishing
15 Alamy/©Colin Underhill

INDEX

INDEX